Environmental Issues

Prospects and Problems

Timely Reports to Keep
Journalists, Scholars and the Public
Abreast of Developing Issues, Events and Trends

Editorial Research Reports
Published by Congressional Quarterly Inc.
1414 22nd Street, N.W.
Washington, D.C. 20037

About the Cover

The cover was illustrated by Guy Aceto and designed by Art Director Richard Pottern.

Editor, Hoyt Gimlin
Managing Editor, Sandra Stencel
Editorial Assistants, Laurie De Maris, Nancy Blanpied
Production Manager, I. D. Fuller
Assistant Production Manager, Maceo Mayo

Library of Congress Cataloging in Publication Data
Main entry under title:

Editorial research reports on environmental issues.

Bibliography: p.
Includes index.
Contents: Closing the environmental decade — Agricultural pesticides — Access to federal lands — [etc.]
1. Environmental policy — United States. 2. United States — Politics and government — 1981-   . I. Congressional Quarterly, inc. II. Title: Environmental issues.
HC110.E5E3   363.7'00973   82-4975
ISBN 0-87187-238-2   AACR2

Contents

Foreword

The environmental movement has been a pervasive force in American life for nearly two decades and, as William Sweet writes in this book's final report, "Americans are unlikely to revert . . . to the habits of an era in which the quality of their air, water and land received little or no attention." But as the 1980s began, environmentalists realized that they would have to adapt to a period in which the chief public concerns were inflation, unemployment and economic stagnation. Opinion polls still registered strong public support for cleaning up the environment, but increasingly people were beginning to ask: How clean? How fast? At what cost?

The fear that environmental concerns would fare badly in the 1980s heightened after Ronald Reagan's election as president. Having worked hard for the enactment of a wide-range of environmental legislation in the 1970s, environmental activists now faced an administration committed to restricting the power of federal agencies and easing the impact of their regulations on business and industry. The president and his appointees also shifted the government's public lands policy away from preservation toward natural resource exploration and development.

The environmental movement's unhappiness with Reagan's policies was made clear in a report published March 31, 1982, by 10 of the nation's leading environmental groups. "President Reagan has broken faith with the American people on environmental protection. . . ," the report said. "Administration officials are handing over to private use the clean air and water, forests, grasslands, coal and oil that belong to us all. In the name of 'getting the government off our backs,' they are giving away our natural heritage."

The report represented a shift in strategy by the environmental movement, which previously had focused their attacks on members of the administration rather than the president himself. Much of their criticism was directed at Interior Secretary James G. Watt. Popular opinion against Watt was demonstrated in October 1981, when environmental groups presented to Congress more than a million petition signatures demanding the secretary's ouster.

Almost as unpopular with environmentalists was Anne M. Gorsuch, head of the Environmental Protection Agency. Gorsuch and her top administrators tried to change EPA's adversary approach towards industry to one of mutual cooperation and to grant states more responsibility for enforcement of pollution control laws.

Environmental groups claim that Reagan's appointments and policies have generated more interest and concern in environmental issues than they've seen since the early 1970s. Environmentalists now are trying to mobilize public opinion against an industry-backed rewrite of the Clean Air Act. Congress also is considering a controversial proposal by Secretary Watt to close the nation's wilderness areas to oil and mineral development for the next 18 years, possible changes in federal pesticide law and in the Endangered Species Act, which is up for reauthorization this year.

The eight reports included in this book discuss the background of these and other environmental problems the nation is likely to face in the years ahead.

Sandra Stencel
Managing Editor

Washington, D.C.
June 1982

Access to Federal Lands

by

Tom Arrandale

Sept. 18
1 9 8 1

Editor's Note: Interior Secretary James G. Watt announced Feb. 21, 1982, that he would seek enactment of a bill to close the nation's wilderness areas to oil and mineral development until the end of the century. The announcement represented a policy reversal for Watt, who had long advocated opening more wilderness to oil and mineral leasing as soon as possible.

Environmental groups, who initially applauded Watt's proposal, changed their tune when draft copies of the legislation leaked out of the Interior Department. Because the measure was silent on the question of what would become of wilderness areas after the year 2000, they feared it would lift wilderness protections after that date. The Wilderness Society labeled the plan "a massive public relations deception" that exchanged "short-term protection for long-term destruction."

ACCESS TO FEDERAL LANDS

S INCE the frontier closed, the United States has been weighing what to do with a splendid heritage of land in the American West. For nearly a century, the federal government has debated the merits of tapping rich public resources or preserving magnificent wilderness. Now James G. Watt, President Reagan's outspoken secretary of the interior, may be forcing a showdown in the historic conflict between putting the nation's resources to use and saving the land for the future.

The outcome could determine the West's destiny — and influence the whole country's well-being. Over the last 20 years, under Republican and Democratic presidents alike, the government has moved to protect national parks, forests, rangelands and offshore waters from abuse while managing them for multiple uses. Since white settlers moved west, the Rocky Mountain and Pacific Coast regions have produced gold, silver, beef and timber in abundance from federally owned lands and shipped them to the rest of the nation. Now, in the past decade, rising petroleum prices have begun pressuring the government to develop vast reserves of coal, oil shale and other energy resources beneath these lands.

President Reagan took office in January pledging to revive the U.S. economy. Since then Watt has been leading a drive to ease or discard federal land and environmental rules that restrict the use of public resources. Watt, a 43-year-old lawyer from Wyoming who had spent 15 years in the Washington bureaucracy, has promised a "common-sense approach to the use and preservation of these lands."[1]

Many Westerners concur with Watt that federal laws enacted in recent years have resulted in costly lawsuits and lengthy environmental studies, stalling public resource development. But Watt's plans to curb national park expansion, open Rocky Mountain wilderness to mineral exploration and encourage more West Coast offshore oil drilling have convinced conservationists — including many Westerners — that the administration intends to go too far toward speeding resource development. "Everybody was startled at how quickly and how vociferously Watt has attacked everything that represents con-

[1] Interview on public television's "The MacNeil/Lehrer Report," WNET/Thirteen, New York, May 20, 1981.

3

servation," commented Deborah Cease, public lands specialist in the Sierra Club's office in Washington, D.C.

During eight months in office, Watt has moved aggressively to apply his own view of conservation to the 400 million acres of land, mostly in the West, that the Interior Department administers for the federal government. Attacking "extreme environmentalists" for opposing resource projects, he has vowed to "swing the pendulum back to center" from the preservationist tack the department has taken in recent years in managing national parks, wildlife refuges and rangelands. As chairman of the President's Cabinet Council on Natural Resources and the Environment, Watt is shaping pro-growth approaches to clean air standards, natural gas pricing, national forest lumbering and other resource decisions by federal agencies.

"The key to conservation is management," Watt told the North American Wildlife and Natural Resoures Conference in Washington, D.C., on March 23. "Conservation is not the blind locking away of huge areas and their resources because of emotional appeals." Watt, accordingly, has ordered Interior officials to push resource projects in Western forests, on rangelands and under offshore waters previously off-limits to development.

James Watt: the Center of Controversy

Watt's initiatives have embroiled him in controversy. California officials, including Democratic Gov. Edmund G. "Jerry" Brown Jr. and both Republican and Democratic members of the state's congressional delegations, protested Watt's announcement in February that he planned to lease four Pacific Ocean basins off the northern California coast for oil. Conservationists objected to Watt's proposal to ease restrictions on access to 25 million acres of public land in the West that Interior's Bureau of Land Management (BLM) is studying for wilderness preservation. Watt's revision of federal strip-mine reclamation standards and reorganization of the department's Office of Surface Mining (OSM) alarmed environmentalists and Congressmen.

Gaylord Nelson, the former Democratic senator from Wisconsin who is chairman of the Wilderness Society, accuses Watt of trying to undo 20 years of bipartisan effort by several presidents and many Congresses to forge a consensus on conservation policies. Addressing members of the Town Hall of California in Los Angeles on Sept. 10, Nelson said:

> Mr. Watt has created a nationwide controversy with his repeated assertions that vast resources of minerals, gas and oil are "locked up" on public lands because of the influence of perverse environmentalists' onerous rules and regulations, bad laws ... and general bad management.... Not unexpectedly, a whole platoon of oil, coal, timber and mining companies have jumped into the fray endorsing his policies and praising his wisdom.

Congressional protests arose over the secretary's plan to halt land purchases to expand national parks and wildlife refuges and use the funds to maintain existing parks instead. Watt's decisions to stop listing new endangered species for federal protection, to impose stiff fees for adopting wild horses and burros rounded up by the government, and to refocus BLM studies of overgrazing on public ranges have also stirred criticism.

"It's been many years and many administrations since a member of a president's Cabinet has drawn flies of controversy like James Watt has done," said public television commentator Jim Lehrer on Aug. 25. "It's been a virtual flap-of-the-week situation for the seven months he has been President Reagan's secretary of the interior."[2] Five days earlier, House Interior Committee Chairman Morris K. Udall, D-Ariz., had declared that "the country would be better off if he [Watt] was gone."

But the president, at a news conference at his California ranch shortly before ending his August vacation, was quick to defend Watt. Indeed, Watt's selection as secretary of the interior was a signal that Reagan considered his 1980 election sweep of the Western states as a mandate for reversing the environmental-minded policies of Cecil D. Andrus, the former Idaho governor who was President Carter's secretary of the interior.

From 1977 until his appointment by Reagan, Watt had served as president of the Mountain States Legal Foundation, a Denver-based public interest law firm financed by Colorado brewer Joseph Coors and some other Rocky Mountain businessmen. In

---

[2] Introduction to the "MacNeil/Lehrer Report," Aug. 25, 1981.

that role, Watt pressed lawsuits against many Interior Department policies that he contended blocked the region's economic progress. In the foundation's 1979-80 annual report, Watt attacked "the extreme environmentalists and the immovable machinery of the bureaucracy" for slowing or stopping energy projects on public lands "at nearly every turn."[3] With Watt and like-minded Westerners now holding key federal resource positions, "the West got ... a group of officials who have made careers fighting the agencies they now direct and resisting the laws they are now charged with enforcing," wrote Wallace Stegner, the author and conservationist.[4]

Secretary Watt

Despite the misgivings of conservationists, the Senate confirmed Watt's appointment Jan. 22 by an 83-12 vote. Since then, however, the secretary's actions and sometimes pugnacious statements not only have enraged environmentalists but sometimes offended key members of Congress and dismayed government resource professionals.

Watt's attitudes, as much as his policies, disturb conservationists who contend that the interior secretary should be the nation's principal defender of wilderness and the environment. In remarks to the Conference of National Park Concessioners in March, Watt recalled being bored during a raft trip down the Colorado River through the Grand Canyon. Backpackers and hikers took offense at his preference for camping in a van and traveling into Wyoming's Wind River Mountains on a snowmobile.

Environmental and Congressional Foes

"This is a man who was nominated for his job in part because he is a Westerner, and yet his insensitivity to the beauty and adventure of the West is appalling," Nathaniel P. Reed, former assistant secretary of the interior under Presidents Nixon and Ford, told a Sierra Club dinner in San Francisco on May 2. Reed, arguing that Watt was betraying the Republican Party's long commitment to conservation, went on to declare him "utterly lacking in the vision and judgment necessary to continue as secretary of the interior."

---

[3] Before moving to Denver to head the foundation, Watt worked in Washington for 15 years, as (1) aide to Sen. Milward Simpson, R-Wyo., as (2) director of Interior's Bureau of Outdoor Recreation, and (3) as a member of the Federal Power Commission.
[4] See Wallace Stegner, "If the Sagebrush Rebels Win, Everybody Loses," *The Living Wilderness,* summer 1981, p. 30.

The Sierra Club launched a petition drive to demand that Watt be ousted. Other wildlife and environmental groups have joined in calling for Watt's dismissal. These include the Izaak Walton League and the National Wildlife Federation, representing fishermen and hunters. "The backlash is just beginning," Wildlife Federation Executive Vice President Jay D. Hair has declared. "It's time for us to fight," National Audobon Society President Russell W. Peterson told the group's biennial convention in July, at which Reagan administration spokesman John B. Crowell Jr. was often hissed and booed.

So far, congressional opposition and court decisions have stalled Watt's most controversial plans. U.S. District Court Judge Mariana Pfaelzer, ruling in Los Angeles July 27 on a lawsuit brought by California officials, barred Interior from leasing drilling rights to 29 tracts in four offshore Pacific basins over the state's objections. Congress rebuffed Watt's request to divert $105 million in offshore oil revenues from the Land and Water Conservation Fund sent up to finance park and refuge expansion. And the House Interior Committee in May directed the secretary to halt plans for oil drilling in three Montana wilderness areas.[5]

Most of Watt's orders to Interior officials will take time to translate into actual land management decisions. "There's a long train of events between proclamations delivered by the secretary and actual changes," said former BLM Director Frank Gregg, now an associate of the Washington-based Conservation Foundation. "We don't know yet what is actually going to happen out there" on Western public lands.[6]

Responding to the 'Sagebrush Rebellion'

If Watt does change public land policy to his liking, Gregg added, "it would be extremely damaging to the public interest, including the interests of the Western states and the people out there." Many Westerners agree, contending that Watt's policies are unpopular among residents of the region's fast-growing cities who hunt, fish, ski and hike in national parks, forests and on public range lands. Sen. James A. McClure, an Idaho Republican and Watt ally who heads the Senate Energy and Natural Resources Committee, privately urged the secretary to tone down his stand, a Senate staff member confided. And White House officials reportedly have told Watt to clear major policy announcements through Reagan's top aides. Some conservationists predict that anxious Republican officials will force Watt's dismissal well before the 1982 congressional elections.

---

[5] See "Western Oil Boom," *E.R.R.*, 1981 Vol. I, pp. 389-408. Attorney General William French Smith told congressional leaders Aug. 6 that the Justice Department would not defend the committee's action against lawsuits brought by Mountain States Legal Foundation, Watt's former employer, and another public-interest firm.

[6] Telephone interview, July 30, 1981.

But Watt still has strong support in the region, especially among Republican senators and state officials, and among ranchers, miners and businessmen who depend on public lands for their livelihood. Sen. Malcolm Wallop, R-Wyo., chairman of the Senate Energy and Natural Resources Committee's Subcommittee on Public Lands, has called Watt "hands-down the first real secretary of the interior that the country has had in a couple of decades." The administration's resource policies in fact respond to resentments that had been building up in the West, especially in Alaska and the Rocky Mountain region, against increased federal government restrictions on its lands and resources.

Those feelings broke out two years ago in the "Sagebrush Rebellion," a protest sparked by the Nevada Legislature's demand that the U.S. government turn over to the state all 48 million acres of Interior Department lands that BLM manages within Nevada's borders. That movement spoke for a host of complaints about BLM policies, including livestock grazing cutbacks, mining and drilling restrictions, wild horse and burro protection, and complicated, slow-moving management procedures. Watt, in Senate confirmation hearings testimony Jan. 7, blamed the rebellion on "the arrogant attitude by [BLM] land managers who refuse to consult with state and local officials and land users."

Watt's mission is "to pacify the West," Sen. Paul Laxalt, a Nevada Republican and close friend of President Reagan, told writer Elizabeth Drew.[7] During his confirmation hearings, Watt told the Senate that "some good management will handle those problems" without transferring federal lands to Western control. Some Western observers think that Watt's hard-line attack on environmentalist positions has been deliberately calculated to defuse rebellious sentiment.

Western enthusiasm for Nevada's revolt has ebbed in the last year, as environmentalists, outdoor sports groups and others rallied against transferring public lands, which they themselves use, to state control and possibly private ownership. While the Arizona, New Mexico, Utah and Wyoming legislatures have gone on record voicing sentiments similar to Nevada's, governors of Colorado and South Dakota have vetoed "sagebrush" measures and the Idaho and Montana legislatures have defeated such proposals.

Leaders of the Nevada rebellion lament that Watt's efforts have taken the steam out of their movement. The secretary wrote Western governors during his second week on the job

---

[7] See Elizabeth Drew, "Secretary Watt," *The New Yorker*, May 4, 1981, p. 104.

offering to exchange small parcels of federal land to give Western cities and towns room for expansion. He also has been negotiating with Utah Gov. Scott M. Matheson, Democrat, to settle a long-pending claim by that state to federal lands within its borders.

Watt's attempts to open public lands for mineral exploration and his approval of streamlined grazing procedures also may mollify important Western interests. "Watt's defused the rebellion by two actions: the new range policy and the steps to identify public lands for community expansion," said Larry Woodard, BLM's associate state director in New Mexico. Watt obviously agreed that he has taken the heat out of the rebellion. He told the Western governors at their 1981 meeting at Jackson Hole, Wyo., Sept. 11, he was now "a rebel without a cause."

"He's defused the movement, and also focused it on a legitimate sagebrush rebellion issue," said Louis D. Higgs, of Albuquerque, N.M., executive director of the Four Corners Regional Commission. "They're getting away from turning land over to the states onto how we can get a more balanced decision-making process."

Managing Western Lands

HOW THE Interior Department manages public lands has long been a vital matter to the West. The department supervises more than 400 million acres of land, roughly one-fifth of the nation's surface, and controls resource development on roughly a billion acres of federal offshore seabeds and on 370 million acres of private holdings, national forests and lands managed by other federal agencies.

It is estimated that 80 percent of the nation's oil shale deposits are on federal lands, as are 35 percent of its uranium reserves, 60 percent of the Western low-sulfur coal and much of the oil and gas now being found from the Overthrust Belt formations that lie beneath Rocky Mountain forests and arid range lands along the Continental Divide.[8] "In the future of federal land and resources law lies a good part of the nation's future welfare," write law professors George C. Coggins of the University of Kansas and Charles F. Wilkinson of the University of Oregon, in a newly published textbook.[9]

---

[8] See U.S. Department of the Interior, Bureau of Land Management, *Public Land Statistics, 1979.*
[9] George C. Coggins and Charles F. Wilkinson, *Federal Public Land and Resources Law* (1981).

   U.S. resource and environmental policies have their most immediate impact in Alaska and in 11 Western states where federal lands are concentrated. Most Interior holdings, like most of the 187 million acres of national forests managed by the Agriculture Department's U.S. Forest Service, lie in the Rocky Mountain and Pacific Coast states, the last parts of the country to be settled. Westerners long have been accustomed to free access to federal lands and use of their valuable resources. But as Congress enlarged the nation's commitment to conservation over the years, the government charged the Forest Service and Interior agencies with multiple and often conflicting goals.

   Interior's National Park Service administers 300 national parks and monuments, about 70 million acres in all, to preserve scenery and wildlife while offering Americans a chance to visit and view them. In 1980, the service reported 300 million visits. Its Fish and Wildlife Service supervises 400 wildlife refuges, protects endangered species, but also traps coyotes and other predators. The department protects wild and scenic rivers; but its Water and Power Resources Administration, formerly the Bureau of Reclamation, builds and operates dams to store water for irrigation and electric power generation.

   Among other Interior agencies: the U.S. Geological Survey studies mineral reserves; the Bureau of Mines studies mining techniques; the Office of Surface Mining interprets and applies federal strip-mine reclamation standards; and the Bureau of Indian Affairs oversees the federal government's role as trustee of Native American reservations.

   And biggest of all is the Bureau of Land Management. Though little-known in the East, Midwest and South, it manages nearly 175 million acres of public domain in the West — plus 76 million acres in Alaska — that are not set aside for specific purposes. The bureau leases to Western ranchers the rights to graze 3.5 million cattle and sheep on the public range. It also rounds up 5,000 wild horses and burros a year and tries to increase forage and improve wildlife habitat on lands that have been abused by decades of overgrazing. "No single federal or state agency manages more wildlife habitat than BLM," William E. Nothdurft, a former bureau official, has noted.[10]

   Those varied mandates make the Interior Department, along with the Forest Service, among the most controversial government agencies. While setting public resource policy goals, Congress has given department officials broad discretion on how to reach them. Their decisions determine which persons can use

<hr>

[10] William E. Nothdurft, "The Lands Nobody Wanted," *The Living Wilderness,* summer 1981, p. 18.

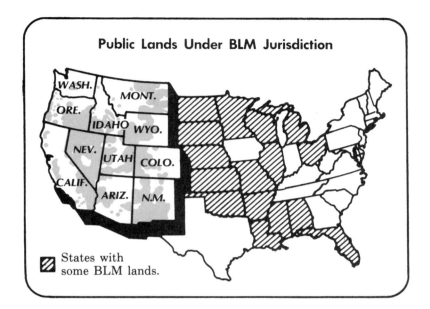

Public Lands Under BLM Jurisdiction

States with some BLM lands.

public lands, and for what activities — with direct consequences for the daily lives and economic prospects of states and communities all over the West.

Frontier Mentality vs. Conservationism

That conflict is a legacy from America's age-old struggle to come to terms with the land. When Europeans first settled North America, the entire continent was primitive wilderness little touched by the Native American peoples who lived here. So long as the frontier was open, colonists and pioneers viewed the land, its wildlife and native inhabitants as a hostile country to be conquered and put to use. "Constant exposure to wilderness gave rise to fear and hatred on the part of those who had to fight it for survival and success," Roderick Nash noted in *Wilderness and the American Mind*.[11]

Those attitudes guided U.S. government land policy as settlement spread west to the territories the nation acquired in the 19th century. Eager to populate the land, the government sold and gave away more than a billion acres to homesteaders, railroads, land speculators, miners and lumberers, schools and governments in the newly formed states. Not until near the end of the century did the government begin setting parks and forests aside for permanent federal management.[12]

Support for conserving Western lands developed first in the East, among dwellers of long-settled cities and towns. Writers like Ralph Waldo Emerson, James Fenimore Cooper and Walt

[11] Roderick Nash, *Wilderness and the American Mind* (1967). Nash is professor of history and environmental studies at the University of California at Santa Barbara.
[12] See "Western Land Policy," *E.R.R.*, 1978 Vol. I, pp. 81-100.

Whitman celebrated the continent's wild beauty; artists George Catlin, John James Audubon, Alexander Wilson and Thomas Cole traveled the frontier painting Indians, wildlife and landscapes. Henry David Thoreau advocated preserving some wilderness for the good of the human mind in a country that was rapidly being converted into farms and urban settings. Most Westerners, however, continued to view the land as a resource to be exploited by plowing, grazing, mining or timbercutting.

In the decades after the Civil War, the government began responding to fears that the last vestiges of the West's scenic grandeur and productive forests were close to being ruined. In 1864, President Abraham Lincoln ceded California's Yosemite Valley to the state for protection in a park; and President Grant in 1872 signed a law designating two million acres in northwestern Wyoming for preservation as Yellowstone National Park.[13] The crusade for wilderness gathered strength in the West, notably California,where it was led by Sierra Club founder John Muir, who was instrumental in the creation of Yosemite National Park in 1890.

In the 1891 General Revision Act, Congress authorized the president to withdraw Western forests from homesteading or other disposal laws to conserve timber and protect watersheds. President Cleveland outraged Westerners in 1897 by establishing 13 new forest reserves across the region. Congress responded by opening the federal forests to use for grazing, mining, timber cutting and other activities.

Roosevelt-Pinchot Era; 1934 Taylor Act

But President Theodore Roosevelt established more national forests, protected the Grand Canyon, and created more national parks and wildlife refuges. Roosevelt also backed the forestry management policies established by Gifford Pinchot. Pinchot, who founded the Forest Service within the Agriculture Department, leased grazing rights on national forests, put timber up for bid and pioneered multiple-use management to make use of forest resources while guarding against abuses that would ruin them for future generations.

In the Taylor Grazing Act of 1934, Congress authorized the Interior Department to regulate livestock use of public lands outside the parks and forests. Many of the lands had been heavily overgrazed. But Western congressional delegations kept the U.S. Grazing Service and its successor, BLM, poorly funded and staffed; and the department remained responsive to the wishes of ranchers and miners.

[13] See "National Park Centennial," *E.R.R.*, 1972 Vol. I, pp. 125-144.

Access to Federal Lands

In the early 1960s, under Interior Secretary Stewart L. Udall, Congress finally directed BLM to follow multiple-use management policies. In the late 1960s and throughout the 1970s the department began applying to public land management a host of federal laws that protected endangered species and free-roaming horses and burros, required environmental impact statements on major government actions, changed federal coal and offshore oil leasing procedures, set federal strip mining regulations, enlarged national parks and wildlife refuges, created a federal wilderness system and generally committed the country to preserving as well as using public lands.

At the same time, the Sierra Club, Wilderness Society and National Wildlife Federation — joined by recently created groups like Friends of the Earth, Natural Resources Defense Council (NRDC) and Environmental Defense Fund — lobbied for more conservationist public-land management and began taking the government to court to force officials to enforce environmental laws more vigorously.

Western Protests Since 1976 Policy Law

Those trends culminated in 1976, when Congress passed the National Forest Management Act and the Federal Land Policy and Management Act (FLPMA). The act essentially ratified the multiple-use policies that the Forest Service and BLM had been pursuing. Long before, Westerners by and large had accepted the Forest Service's role in conserving timber and water resources. But FLPMA, also known as the BLM Organic Act, stirred widespread resentment among ranchers, miners and others who for decades had used public lands with little supervision.

The law confirmed and strengthened the bureau's powers to draw up long-term management plans. The measure directed the bureau to identify roadless public lands that still could be preserved as part of the national wilderness system. It formally reversed the 19th century land disposal laws, declaring that the nation would hold onto the leftover public domain and manage it for national purposes. The law gave BLM permanent standing and encouraged its staff to proceed with planning to conserve range, watersheds, minerals, wildlife, recreation and public land forests according to the staff's professional judgment.

As their authority has grown, both BLM and the Forest Service have adopted elaborate procedures for drafting management plans for the lands they administer. BLM enlarged its field staffs, adding wildlife biologists, archeologists, recreation planners, wilderness specialists and other specialists to recommend that district managers take steps to protect such noncommercial resources. Those changes were taking hold as President Carter took office in 1977 and were identified with his administration. Moreover, he angered Western interests by trying to cut back spending on federal dam-building projects in the region. At the same time, Secretary of the Interior Andrus alarmed public land users by filling middle-level Interior Department posts with persons who formerly worked for environmentalist groups.

Western hostility finally flared into the Sagebrush Rebellion. Few observers give claims to federal lands by Western state governments much chance of success in either federal courts or Congress. And Arizona's Democratic Gov. Bruce Babbitt dismisses the rebellion's leaders as "the same old special-interest crowd that has been grabbing for Western land [since] the days of Teddy Roosevelt."[14] Yet the West's revolt — and Watt's campaign to redress its grievances — has drawn national attention to serious questions that remain un-

Governor Babbitt

resolved about managing federally owned lands and resources.

Balancing the Use of Public Resources

Over the last 20 years, "we've seen the process which leads to resource use complicated to the point where it's almost unmanageable," said Elwood Miller, a University of Nevada (at Reno) professor of forestry.[15] The 1976 laws guiding BLM and Forest Service planning require extensive consultations with the public, including local governments, land users and environmentalists, before decisions are put into effect. The federal Endangered Species Act and the National Environmental Policy Act (NEPA) of 1969 often force lengthy studies of public lands and their wildlife before resource development is authorized.[16]

Early in the 1970s, environmental groups and public-interest law firms became skillful at using court challenges to environmental impact statements — that had been prepared by the agencies — to delay proposed projects and marshal public backing for land preservation. And by the end of the decade, public land users, businessmen and conservative organizations like Watt's Mountain States Legal Foundation had discovered that

---

[14] Quoted by Stegner, *op. cit.*, p. 32.
[15] Telephone interview, July 20, 1981.
[16] See "Environmental Policy," *E.R.R.*, 1974 Vol. II, pp. 945-964, and "Closing the Environmental Decade," *E.R.R.*, 1979 Vol. II, pp. 821-840.

they also could use court actions to force reconsideration of public land management decisions.[17]

During Andrus' tenure, Interior officials tried to forge a consensus among environmentalists and resource users to head off costly litigation. As BLM director, Gregg began reviewing the bureau's procedures for assessing livestock grazing damage to public range to give ranchers a greater role in the process. The department also revised federal coal leasing procedures and worked to expedite power-plant sitings and offshore oil and gas leasing.

But in some cases, at least, Interior officials acknowledge that the department was too hesitant during Carter's term about pushing development over environmentalist opposition. "We could have streamlined the policy process, cut the time frame down significantly," said Joellen Murphy, former BLM deputy director for policy analysis. "Sometimes we didn't fight court decisions that environmentalists had won that we probably should have appealed," she added in an interview. When Watt took over, "there were an awful lot of people in the bureau who were anxious to get going again," Murphy went on, "but we've all been fired."

Conflicts Over Production

WATT HAS dismissed or demoted many holdover Interior officials, replacing Gregg as BLM director with Colorado rancher Robert L. Burford, former Speaker of that state's House of Representatives, whose family holds a permit to graze cattle on bureau range lands. Reagan named another conservative Colorado legislator, Denver attorney Anne McGill Gorsuch, as head of the Environmental Protection Agency (EPA).

Other key administration officials — including Office of Surface Mining Director James R. Harris and Assistant Secretary of Agriculture John B. Crowell Jr., a former timber company attorney who now supervises the Forest Service — were critics of Carter's resource policies. Through budget cutbacks and agency reorganizations, the administration also has reduced Interior Department commitments to wildlife, recreation and archeological preservation while putting funds into expediting resource development.

---

[17] See Richard R. Liroff, "NEPA Litigation in the 1970s," *Natural Resources Journal*, April 1981, p. 315.

During the next three years, Reagan officials can be expected to apply their production philosophy to a host of pending resource decisions. Writing in the July 1981 issue of the *Enterprise,* magazine of the National Association of Manufacturers, the secretary argued that the nation must inventory the resources that the public lands hold in order to make wise decisions. "Failure to know our potential, to inventory our resources — intentionally forbidding proper access to needed resources — limits this nation, dooms us to decline. . . ."

Pending Decisions on Land Resources

Watt has followed up by reviewing the BLM wilderness study that Congress ordered in 1976. The department has already relaxed the rules that had been written to prevent environmental damage by drilling on the 24 million acres that the bureau identified as potential wilderness in 1980. The drilling was permitted by previous leases. Officials have weighed redrawing boundaries and changing the definition of a road in ways that would reduce the amount of land under consideration. And Watt has considered asking Congress to release for development other areas that BLM had surveyed for potential wilderness but ruled out as unsuitable.

Wilderness advocates contend that the bureau overlooked some areas that deserve protection, and they object to relaxing interim management rules to prevent disturbance in those areas before Congress can consider what to do about them. The administration also is backing legislation introduced by Sen. S. I. "Sam" Hayakawa, R-Calif., to set deadlines for Congress to act on Forest Service proposals to add 15 million acres of forest lands to the wilderness system and study 12 million other acres of roadless areas for possible preservation.

The Hayakawa measure also would release for multiple-use management 36 million acres that the Forest Service found unqualified during the Carter administration's Roadless Area Review and Evaluation (RARE II). The study was an effort to resolve longstanding conflicts over what remaining lands should be added to the wilderness system. Congress has been considering RARE II proposals on a state-by-state basis, and in 1980 it passed laws expanding the national forests' wilderness system by 609,060 acres in New Mexico, 1.4 million acres in Colorado, 2.3 million acres in Idaho and 5.3 million acres in Alaska.[18]

Watt also has considered proposals to extend a deadline that Congress set in the Wilderness Act of 1964 for mineral exploration in wilderness preserves. That law prohibited mineral leas-

---

[18] For background, see "Wilderness Preservation," *E.R.R.*, 1975 Vol. I, pp. 383-402.

Federal Lands in the West
(in acres)

	BLM	Total	% of State
Alaska*	222,235,135	326,925,561	89.5
Arizona	12,588,917	32,014,276	44.0
California	16,609,375	46,702,125	46.6
Colorado	7,993,938	23,607,947	35.5
Idaho	11,945,940	33,759,572	63.8
Montana	8,141,652	27,740,572	29.7
Nevada	48,844,808	60,506,114	86.1
New Mexico	12,840,456	25,873,745	33.3
Oregon	15,745,064	32,313,688	52.5
Utah	22,052,628	33,529,967	63.6
Washington	311,157	12,472,704	29.2
Wyoming	17,793,105	30,329,556	48.7

* Alaska figures have changed under terms of 1980 Alaska lands legislation.
Source: *Public Lands Statistics 1979*, Bureau of Land Management

ing in wilderness regions, beginning in 1984. The deadline is less than three years away, but oil and mining company officials object that federal land agencies have managed designated and potential wilderness areas in ways that have prevented the exploration of large tracts where valuable energy resources and scarce strategic metals might be found.

Watt has indicated sympathy for those complaints and expressed concern that the nation has failed to develop its resources of strategic minerals like chromium, cobalt and titanium. In congressional testimony, he pledged to act as "spokesman for the very real public interest involved in the protection and preservation of a strong minerals sector" in the U.S. economy.

Proposal For Strategic Minerals Policy

In response to those concerns, Rep. James D. Santini, a Nevada Democrat who is chairman of the House Interior Subcommittee on Mines and Mining, has drawn up legislation that calls for a national strategic minerals policy, larger stockpiles of key metals and assessment of what reserves lie beneath federal lands. In a television interview on June 17, Santini argued that wilderness studies and management restrictions had placed 68 percent of the public lands "in practical terms off limits to even looking for what mineral resources we have there."[19]

Former Carter administration officials contend that Interior Department procedures have for years been gradually opening public lands for mineral searches. But Santini's measure would

[19] "The MacNeil/Lehrer Report," June 17, 1981.

extend the 1984 deadline for mineral claims in wilderness regions until 1994 and make mining the dominant use of all public lands holding "significant mineral deposits." Under the measure, "every single acre of public land could, at the whim of Secretary Watt, be drilled and mined — regardless of other values of the land," Terry Sopher of the Wilderness Society has objected. "Even national parks could be declared fair game."[20]

Debate Over National Forest Lumbering

In addition to speeding Interior Department mineral leasing, the Reagan administration also is eager to step up harvests of timber from the nation's national forests, which produce an annual average of 12 billion board feet. The U.S. lumber industry, running out of trees to cut from privately owned lands in the Pacific Northwest, has been lobbying to double the harvest from 89 million acres of commercial timber managed by the Forest Service. Crowell, as general counsel to Louisiana-Pacific Corp., the nation's second-largest timber company,[21] called for accelerated cutting of old-growth stands of trees in the national forests never before harvested.

As Reagan's assistant secretary of agriculture for natural resources and the environment, Crowell has proposed that the Forest Service depart from its policy of not selling more timber than the national forests continue to grow in a given period. Congress endorsed that "non-declining even flow" management in the 1976 National Forest Management Act but gave the service some discretion to increase harvests if it also increased reforestation and other growing efforts. President Carter in 1979 ordered a temporary increase in 1979 in an attempt to lower lumber prices, but timber cutting declined rather than increased because Congress reduced Forest Service funds related to timber production.

Now Crowell is pushing for increased cutting of mature timber — timber that has stopped growing and eventually will die and rot unless harvested. This includes 60 percent of the national forest timber in the Pacific Northwest. "We now have a remarkable opportunity to reduce the potential gap in timber supply in the Northwest," Crowell has said. "I want to make the national forests contribute more to the economic well-being of the country."[22]

Reagan administration plans for resource development, along with lingering Sagebrush Rebellion sentiments, prompt angry

[20] See "Proposed Mining Bill Threatens Wilderness," *The Living Wilderness*, summer 1981, p. 46.
[21] After Weyerhaeuser; Georgia-Pacific ranks third.
[22] Quoted by Lawrence Mosher, "The Nation's Ailing Timber Industry Finds It Has a Friend in Washington," *National Journal*, July 11, 1981, p. 1237.

debate in Washington. But out in the Rocky Mountain states a consensus has started to emerge on developing the region's immense energy reserves without ruining all of its wild and scenic vistas. During Andrus' tenure, environmentalists and businessmen began working out agreement on acceptable resource projects. Conservationists recognized that growth was inevitable, while energy firms began building new towns, providing financial aid to local governments and taking steps to prevent undue ecological damage by their facilities.

Emerging Consensus in Rocky Mountains

At the same time, governors of the Rocky Mountain states organized to shape U.S. resource policies more to their liking. Working through the Denver-based Western Governors Policy Office (WESTPO), 13 governors[23] now are forging common positions to negotiate with Interior and Energy Department officials on the pace and timing of Western resource projects. They argue that federal energy reserves — and massive projects like the MX missile[24] — must proceed by an orderly, phased-in process that gives states and communities time to accommodate growth and prepare a long-term economic base that will remain after the resources are exhausted. But unless Western states respond positively to national energy needs, "there will be a backlash in the near future that will simply ride roughshod over the West,"said WESTPO Executive Director Philip Burgess.

Many Westerners, including Secretary Watt, share that concern. Watt has argued that environmentalists' efforts to delay Western resource development eventually could cause severe energy shortages, forcing the federal government to launch a crash program to tap Western energy. "We have the energy and it's going to be developed," Watt told the annual meeting of the International Association of Fish and Wildlife Agencies in Albuquerque, Sept. 14. "The only questions are when and how."

The WESTPO governors often disagreed with Andrus over public land policy. Eager to establish better relations with Watt, the governors have avoided criticizing his proposals. Some, like Matheson of Utah and Ed Herschler of Wyoming, both Democrats, have praised Watt's efforts. But two other Democratic governors, Richard D. Lamm of Colorado and Babbitt of Arizona, have been alarmed by what they see at Watt's plans to dismantle federal environmental protection standards.

Some Westerners worry that Watt's plans will backfire as environmentalists go to court to block resource projects. If that happens, the backlash could carry federal land policies quickly

[23] Alaska, Arizona, Colorado, Idaho, Montana, Nevada, New Mexico, North Dakota, South Dakota, Utah, Washington and Wyoming.
[24] For background, see "M-X Missile Decision," *E.R.R.*, 1981, Vol. I, pp. 409-428.

back toward the preservation goals that Watt now is attacking. "There has to be a balance," a BLM official commented. "What I worry about is that we never seem to stop in the middle where we should be."

Selected Bibliography

Books

Coggins, George Cameron and Wilkinson, Charles F., *Federal Public Land and Resources Law,* The Foundation Press Inc., 1981.
Nash, Roderick, *Wilderness and the American Mind,* Yale University Press, 1967.
Udall, Stewart L., *The Quiet Crisis,* Holt, Rinehart and Winston, 1963.
Watkins, T. H. and Charles S. Watson Jr., *The Lands No One Knows, America and the Public Domain,* Sierra Club Books, 1975.

Articles

Culhane, Paul J. and H. Paul Friesma, "Land Use Planning for the Public Lands," *Natural Resources Journal,* January 1979.
Drew, Elizabeth, "Secretary Watt," *The New Yorker,* May 4, 1981.
"James Watt's Land Rush," *Newsweek,* June 29, 1981.
Koch, Kathy, "Watt's Clashes With Congress Stall Programs," *Congressional Quarterly Weekly Report,* July 11, 1981.
Liroff, Richard A., "NEPA Litigation in the 1970s: A Deluge or a Dribble?" *Natural Resources Journal,* April 1981.
Mosher, Lawrence, "The Nation's Ailing Timber Industry Finds It has a Friend in Washington," *National Journal,* July 11, 1981, p. 1237.
"Special Public Lands Issue," *The Living Wilderness,* summer 1981, various articles.
Watt, James G., "We Must Inventory Our Lands," *Enterprise,* July 1981.
Wolf, Ron, "New Voice in the Wilderness: James Watt," *Rocky Mountain Magazine,* March-April 1981.

Reports and Studies

Editorial Research Reports: "Wilderness Preservation," 1975 Vol. I, p. 385; "Forest Policy," 1975 Vol. II, p. 867; "Western Land Policy," 1978 Vol. I, p. 83; "Western Oil Boom," 1981 Vol. I, p. 391.
General Accounting Office, "Land Use Issues," June 27, 1980.
Public Land Law Review Commission, "One Third of the Nation's Land," June 1970.
U.S. Department of the Interior Bureau of Land Management, *Public Land Statistics, 1979.*

Cover art and p. 11 map by Staff Artist Robert Redding. Cartoon on p. 5 by Doug Marlette of *The Charlotte Observer.*

A IR POLLUTION CONTROL: PROGRESS AND PROSPECTS

by

William Sweet

**Nov. 21
1 9 8 0**

Editor's Note: Although the Clean Air Act technically expired on Sept. 30, 1981, Senate and House committees made little progress in rewriting the bill last year, and funding for continued enforcement of the law was provided through appropriations resolutions. Debate over revision of air regulations got underway in earnest during winter 1982, when Rep. Thomas A. Luken, D-Ohio, introduced a bill — HR 5252 — that would significantly weaken current rules.

Environmental groups launched a vigorous grassroots campaign against HR 5252, but the proposed bill was backed by a bipartisan majority of the House Health and Environmental Subcommittee, led by Rep. John D. Dingell, D-Mich., chairman of the full Energy and Commerce Committee. On March 24, the subcommittee passed a version of HR 5252 that would relax emission on standards for automobiles and factories, extend deadlines for states to meet national clean air standards, reduce visibility protection around national parks and eliminate a ban on new construction in dirty air areas.

In an apparent effort to confuse environmentalists, the subcommittee changed the number of the bill it adopted to HR 5555, the number that was originally attached to a contrary bill sponsored by Rep. Henry A. Waxman, D-Calif. — the leading opponent of HR 5252. Waxman's strategy is to delay final action on clean air revisions until later in the year. Since public support for strong clean air rules is high, Waxman expects politicians to become more reluctant to gut the Clean Air Act as election day approaches.

AIR POLLUTION CONTROL: PROGRESS AND PROSPECTS

CLEAN AIR legislation, the most far-reaching and costly of the pollution abatement laws enacted during the 1970s, comes up for renewal in 1981.[1] Until recently, environmental lobbyists expressed confidence that changes in the clean air laws would be minor. Representatives of industries affected by the laws seemed to agree. But with the election of Ronald Reagan as president and the defeat of many Democrats in House and Senate races, all bets are off. After Jan. 20, the White House will be occupied by a man who has promised to re-write the clean air laws in collaboration with industry. In Congress, the balance of power will shift to the advantage of those who believe government regulations of all kinds must be cut.

At the Democratic National Convention last summer, Sen. Edward M. Kennedy, D-Mass., aroused peals of laughter when he quoted Reagan as saying that "80 percent of our air pollution comes from plants and trees."[2] Most of the delegates no doubt assumed this was a statement Reagan would prefer to forget. But speaking Oct. 7 in Steubenville, Ohio, Reagan reminded his supporters of Kennedy's remarks and defended his original position: "First of all, I didn't say 80 percent. I said 92 percent — pardon me, 93 percent. And I didn't say air pollution; I said oxides of nitrogen. And I am right. Growing and decaying vegetation in this land are responsible for 93 percent of the oxides of nitrogen." In the same speech, Reagan said he suspected that the eruption of Mount St. Helens had released more sulfur dioxide into the air in just a few months "than has been released in the last 10 years of automobile driving or things of that kind. . . ." Later that day, Reagan told an audience in Youngstown, Ohio, that air pollution "has been substantially controlled."

The same day Reagan was promising Ohio audiences that he would revise clean air laws in consultation with the coal and steel industries, the Los Angeles area was in the second week of the worst smog episode in recent memory.[3] Carter

---

[1] Congress in 1977 authorized $200 million a year, covering the period 1978-1981, for implementation and enforcement of the Clean Air Act of 1970 and the Clean Air Amendments of 1977 (see p. 26). Re-authorization, often a routine matter, can be an occasion for critics of the legislation to offer amendments.

[2] Reagan made the statement to which Kennedy referred in a 1979 radio broadcast.

[3] Smog forms when the sun's ultraviolet rays trigger a chemical reaction between hydrocarbons and nitrogen dioxide. The reactions give rise to a number of secondary pollutants including ozone, aldehydes and benzopyrene.

officials lost no time in taking Reagan to task for his views. Douglas M. Costle, administrator of the Environmental Protection Agency (EPA), said that Reagan had confused nitrogen dioxide, a regulated pollutant, with nitrous oxides, which are harmless products of plant respiration. Gus Speth, chairman of the president's Council on Environmental Quality (CEQ), pointed out that soil bacteria — not trees — are the primary source of nitrous oxides. Calling Reagan's remarks "strange and bewildering," Speth said that human sources emit sulfur dioxide at a rate 40 times as high as Mount St. Helens, and he reminded Americans that power plants — not cars, as Reagan had implied — are the principal source of sulfur pollutants.

Reagan's misstatements about air pollution and his record on air quality issues made Carter the favored presidential candidate of most environmental groups, once Kennedy and Gov. Edmund G. Brown Jr. of California were defeated in the primaries. The League of Conservation Voters, a Washington-based organization that rates candidates on environmental issues, gave Carter a "C+" on air quality issues and Reagan an "F." [4] As governor of California (1967-1975), Reagan signed one of the nation's toughest air pollution laws. But in 1971 he blocked enactment of exceptionally strict auto emission controls, and in 1975 he vetoed a bill that would have given Southern California a unified air pollution control authority. In 1974, when the state Air Resources Board tried to implement unpopular regulations requiring cars that were already on the road to be fitted with pollution control devices, Reagan fired two board members and replaced them with people characterized by one California environmentalist as "industry hacks." [5]

Reagan's first significant environmental decisions as president probably will involve the selection of people to head such agencies as the Council on Environmental Quality and the Environmental Protection Agency. Given EPA's broad powers to set and enforce standards, the person Reagan chooses to be his environmental administrator will be subjected to especially close scrutiny. Reagan named Norman Livermore, former director of the National Audubon Society, to head his transition team on environmental affairs. Livermore was director of California's Department of Resources under Reagan.

Reagan may pick some officials from a special environmental task force that he established after his remarks in Ohio caused wide consternation. The task force includes several people who work for conservationist organizations, such as the National Wildlife Federation, the National Audubon Society and the

---

[4] Anderson got a b+, Kennedy an a− and Brown an A. Capital letters indicate leadership on environmental issues, while small letters reflect a more passive voting record.
[5] Carl Pope of the Sierra Club, San Francisco, interview on Nov. 6, 1980.

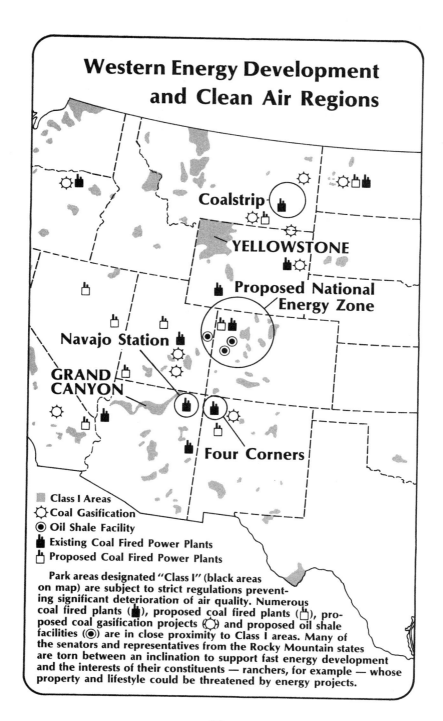

Western Energy Development and Clean Air Regions

Coalstrip

YELLOWSTONE

Proposed National Energy Zone

Navajo Station

GRAND CANYON

Four Corners

- ▦ Class I Areas
- ✿ Coal Gasification
- ◉ Oil Shale Facility
- ▟ Existing Coal Fired Power Plants
- ⌂ Proposed Coal Fired Power Plants

Park areas designated "Class I" (black areas on map) are subject to strict regulations preventing significant deterioration of air quality. Numerous coal fired plants (▟), proposed coal fired plants (⌂), proposed coal gasification projects (✿) and proposed oil shale facilities (◉) are in close proximity to Class I areas. Many of the senators and representatives from the Rocky Mountain states are torn between an inclination to support fast energy development and the interests of their constituents — ranchers, for example — whose property and lifestyle could be threatened by energy projects.

Sierra Club, as well as two respected environmental officials from earlier Republican administrations — Russell Train and William Ruckelshaus.[6] The task force submitted a report to Reagan in early November. While the report's contents still are confidential, it was reported to have recommended relaxation of clean air deadlines and greater use of tax incentives as a means of encouraging companies to comply with air regulations.

1970 Clean Air Act and 1977 Amendments

In addition to exercising discretionary powers in the area of environmental regulation, the officials chosen by Reagan will play a key role in recommending and commenting on proposed revisions of clean air legislation. The nation's fundamental rules for controlling air pollution were established in the Clean Air Act of 1970, which required the Environmental Protection Agency to set national air quality standards for major pollutants. State and local governments were given the task of bringing air into compliance with those standards by whatever procedures proved necessary and acceptable. At the same time, emissions of certain pollutants were required to be reduced at the source — be that automobiles, other modes of transportation, industrial facilities or power plants.

Progress in reaching the goals of the Clean Air Act proved slower than expected, and in 1977 Congress enacted amendments modifying the 1970 objectives. The amendments relaxed several compliance deadlines but also tightened clean air legislation in several important respects. They established three categories of areas with air that is cleaner than required under national standards, specified how much levels of sulfur and dioxide and particulates could increase in each category and required the EPA to propose regulations for "prevention of significant deterioration" — "PSD" — in levels of nitrogen oxide, hydrocarbons, carbon monoxide and photochemical oxidants. The PSD provisions were designed partly to prevent the nation's air from deteriorating to a mediocre national average, and partly to prevent industries from relocating facilities from exceptionally dirty to clean areas *(see box, p. 43)*.

The amendments gave states until July 1, 1979, to complete their revised State Implementation Plans for attainment of ambient air standards and required all plans to contain a permit program for major stationary sources of pollution. In "nonattainment" areas (areas not in compliance with ambient air standards), permits for new industrial facilities and plants would be granted only when additional emissions would be

---

[6] Train served as chairman of the Council on Environmental Quality (1970-1973) and as administrator of the Environmental Protection Agency (1973-1977). Ruckelshaus served as EPA administrator (1970-1973).

"offset" by reductions from other sources. States requesting extension of the deadline for compliance with ambient air standards from 1982 to 1987, because of severe auto-related problems, would be required to establish vehicle inspection and maintenance programs.

The amendments also provided for the establishment of a National Commission on Air Quality, which would conduct a three-year study of national air pollution legislation and then recommend revisions to Congress. The commission originally was supposed to send its final report to Congress in August 1980. But because President Carter was 11 months late in making appointments to the commission, Congress extended its deadline to March 1, 1981. According to Morris A. Ward, the commission's director for public affairs and administration, the final report will discuss such matters as standard setting and permit procedures, "PSD" and non-attainment rules, special issues such as ozone formation and high altitude carbon monoxide, and air problems in certain special regions including Southern California, the New York-Hartford corridor and the Ohio River basin. Ward said the commission would not make judgments about the specific numerical standards set by EPA.[7]

Environmental and Economic Trade-Offs

The 11-member National Commission on Air Quality, chaired by Sen. Gary Hart, D-Colo., includes prominent environmentalists, several members of Congress and representatives of regions and industries specially affected by air quality problems. Its final report is likely to take into account the adverse effects air regulations can have on inflation, employment and economic growth, but it is unlikely to recommend far-reaching relaxation of clean air laws.

The platform that the Republicans adopted in Detroit on July 15 said in its five-paragraph section on the environment that "[m]uch progress has been made in achieving the goals of clean air. . . . At the same time, we believe that it is imperative that environmental laws and regulations be reviewed, and where necessary, reformed to ensure that the benefits achieved justify the costs imposed. . . . We believe, in particular, that regulatory procedures must be reformed to expedite decision making. Endless delay harms both the environment and the economy. We strongly affirm that environmental protection must not become a cover for a 'no-growth' policy and a shrinking economy."

During his campaign, Reagan often attributed the serious problems of the automobile and steel industries to excessive government regulation, and he indicated that the country's

[7] Interview, Oct. 29, 1980.

27

booming coal economy would be even stronger but for environmental rules. In speeches prepared for delivery at Steubenville and Youngstown, Ohio, the day he made his off-the-cuff remarks about trees and Mount St. Helens, Reagan said that "Mr. Carter's EPA appointees apparently don't know and don't care about coal. It's time that we had a president who will see to it that EPA has leaders who understand how vital coal is to the nation and to Ohio's economy." Referring to plans to provide the steel industry with three-year extensions on clean air deadlines on a case-by-case basis, a program Carter announced on Sept. 31, Reagan said "Carter only rediscovered the needs of steel one month before the election. I won't wait three and a half years to help the steel industry." Calling the steel industry "one of the most overregulated industries in America," Reagan said he would stretch out compliance times for all steel companies.

According to the American Iron and Steel Institute, the steel industry has spent $3.4 billion on pollution control since 1970. Critics of the industry blame its problems on a host of factors — failure to modernize in the face of mounting foreign competition, investment of industry profits in non-steel enterprises, high wage rates, and so on. EPA estimates that pollution control expenditures have driven up steel prices by only 4 percent or so. The steel industry claims the correct figure is closer to 6 percent, and it says many of its problems would be solved by relaxation of air standards.[8]

Coal and utility groups would be equally happy to see standards relaxed. In the Ohio Valley and especially in Ohio itself, where 21 aged coal-fired plants add up to the most concentrated source of sulfur pollutants in the country, utilities have fought hard for exemptions from clean air regulations. In many cases, they have brought coal-fired plants into compliance with ambient air standards — which are enforced on the basis of local ground readings — by building tall stacks. The effect has been to blow sulfur pollutants, a principal source of acid rain, over the eastern parts of the United States and Canada.[9] Local producers of coal fear that strict clean air rules would give an unfair advantage to Western state producers of low sulfur coal.

In the West — where coal-burning plants increasingly export electricity to California and the Midwest and where massive development of synthetic fuels based on coal and oilshale could threaten air quality in countless new ways — many energy corporations are planning projects that could be jeopardized

[8] See Lawrence Mosher, "Big Steel Says It Can't Afford to Make the Nation's Air Pure," *National Journal,* July 5, 1980, pp. 1088-1092.
[9] See "Acid Rain," *E.R.R.,* 1980 Vol. I, pp. 445-464.

by the especially strict clean air restrictions affecting national parks *(see map, p. 25)*.[10] Conflicts over clean air requirements already have arisen in connection with Montana's Coalstrip power plants, which send electricity to the East, and several facilities in the Southwest, which send electricity to the West.[11] One of the more ambitious synfuel projects, a brain-child of Exxon, would involve the construction of 150 processing plants in the northwestern corner of Colorado. According to Exxon Corp. Chairman, C. C. Garwin, the area would have to be declared a "national energy zone" in which "normal rules do not apply."[12]

New Political Alignments

WHEN Congress reviews the clean air laws next year, investor-owned utilities will rely on the Edison Electric Institute, their trade association, to promote their interests.[13] The institute is just one of the industry groups that will be lobbying hard in 1981. The American Petroleum Institute, the Chemical Manufacturers Association, the Iron and Steel Institute, the American Paper Institute, the American Automobile Association and countless more will be promoting the interests of their industries in the halls of Congress, at EPA and in executive offices.

In addition to these individual trade groups, four well-known business organizations — the Business Roundtable, the U.S. Chamber of Commerce, the National Association of Manufacturers (NAM) and the National Environmental Development Association (NEDA) — are preparing detailed positions on clean air revisions *(See box, p. 30)*. Of these, NEDA may be the most influential voice in next year's deliberations. Among other

---

[10] On June 16, 1980, Senate and House conferees reached agreement on a $20-billion synthetic fuels bill. The bill, signed by President Carter on June 30, established an Energy Security Corporation to allocate the funds to private industry. John C. Sawhill, chief of the Federal Energy Administration under Presidents Nixon and Ford, was named head of the seven-member board on Sept. 13. Most scientific authorities agree that the facilities currently envisioned to produce oil shale, and coal gasification and liquefaction, will not meet current air pollution standards. "Emissions vary according to the technology," Mark Trautwein of the congressional Environmental Study Conference wrote in 1979, "but very large amounts of particulates, sulfur dioxides, nitrous oxides, hydrocarbons and other pollutants would be released, not only in end-use consumption, but also in mining and at the plant where the coal or shale is converted to synthetic petroleum." See "Synthetic Fuels," *E.R.R.*, 1979 Vol. II, pp. 621-640.

[11] According to Richard Silverman of the Salt River Reclamation Project, a public utility in Arizona, problems have arisen in connection with Nevada's Mohave plant, the Four Corners plant (at the intersection of Arizona, Colorado, New Mexico and Utah) and the Navaho Generating Station at Page, Ariz. Interview, Oct. 30, 1980.

[12] See Janet Marinelli, "Gearing up for Synfuels," *Environmental Action*, November 1980, p. 14.

[13] Some utilities also are members of the Utility Air Regulatory Group (URAG), which represents their interests in administrative rule-making proceedings and in litigation. URAG was founded in March 1970 to oppose a proposed performance standard that would have required removal of 90 percent of the sulfur from all coal plant emissions.

Business Lobbies

In addition to the lobbying efforts mounted by individual corporations and trade associations such as the American Petroleum Institute, four groups representing a variety of businesses have launched programs to promote revision of clean air legislation.

National Environmental Development Association/Clean Air Project. Founded in 1973 to provide information on balancing environmental and economic needs, NEDA organized its air project (CAAP) in March 1979. Participants in the project include the 17 members of the Building and Construction Trades Department of the AFL-CIO and 34 corporations including Exxon, Dow Chemical, General Motors, Kaiser Aluminum, the Union Pacific and Weyerhaeuser. The steering committee of the project, chaired by John Quarles, former general counsel, head of enforcement and deputy administrator of EPA, issued a report Nov. 18 recommending changes in the Clean Air Act.

Business Roundtable. The Roundtable has as members the chief executive officers of 200 large corporations. James H. Evans, chairman of the Union Pacific Corporation, heads the Roundtable's Environmental Task Force, and William J. McDonald, senior vice president for law with the Union Pacific, is coordinating the task force's air studies. Four clean air issues have been singled out for detailed attention: (1) procedures for setting air quality standards, and especially health standards; (2) prevention of significant deterioration; (3) permitting procedures; and (4) analysis of regulatory costs. The studies are in the final stages of review and the target date for board approval is Nov. 20.

U.S. Chamber of Commerce. The chamber has roughly 100,000 members, both individuals and businesses. Its environmental committee expects to recommend changes in clean air legislation to the board of directors in late November. Problems facing firms in non-attainment areas are a top priority, but prevention of deterioration, confusion and delays in the permitting process and unpredictable factors in environmental regulation also rank high. The chamber expects to publish two pamphlets on clean air legislation in mid-December.

National Association of Manufacturers. The 12,000 companies that are NAM members account for roughly 75 percent of U.S. manufacturing capacity. The association is less advanced than the other groups in developing a position on clean air regulations, but it expects to have a report out by March 1, when the National Commission on Air Quality is expected to issue its report *(see p. 27)*. NAM's recommendations are likely to be similar to those advanced by the Chamber of Commerce and the Roundtable.

things, the organization will recommend improving the scientific foundation for air standards, relaxing significant deterioration requirements, abolishing EPA's bans on new construction in non-attainment areas, basing regulations on "best available technology" rather than "lowest achievable emission rates," delaying action on acid rain until more is known about the problem, and giving states greater discretion in modifying their implementation plans.

Depending on their members' interests, the various associations emphasize different aspects of clean air legislation. The U.S. Chamber of Commerce, which has as members many small and medium-sized businesses in the older and dirtier areas of the Northeast and Midwest, devotes a lot of attention to rules affecting non-attainment regions. It also works to simplify regulations and reduce time-consuming paperwork, because, in the words of the chamber's environmental expert, small businesses "don't have the resources that big corporations have to cope with regulation."[14] Organizations representing big business, on the other hand, are working for fundamental revisions of regulations that have a big impact on corporate balance sheets.

Typical of these big companies is the Union Pacific, a leading participant in the Roundtable's clean air effort. No longer merely a railroad, the Union Pacific became a holding company in 1969. Its mining subsidiary, Rocky Mountain Energy, owns vast coal, uranium and soda ash reserves in southern Wyoming, Utah and Colorado. Its multimillion-ton coal reserves in the Great Divide Basin in Wyoming may become a significant source of synthetic fuels, according to the company's 1979 annual report. An oil subsidiary, Champlin Petroleum, owns refineries in Texas, Oklahoma and Southern California and drills for oil all over the West. In 1979, for the first time in the company's history, more than half its earnings — 61 percent — came from energy and natural resources.

Support for Upholding Strict Standards

Arrayed against the industrial associations are a number of environmental, public health and "public interest" groups that would like to see the clean air laws maintained in their essential features and, if possible, strengthened. The Sierra Club, the League of Women Voters, National Parks and Conservation, Friends of the Earth, the Natural Resources Defense Council and the Environmental Defense Fund will be coordinating their efforts as members of the "Clean Air Coalition," which was founded in 1973. According to coordinator Betsy Agle, the coalition is preparing working papers on acid rain and toxic air

[14] Linda Wooley, assistant director for resources and environment, interview, Oct. 27, 1980.

pollutants.[15] Environmentalists have accused EPA of not acting quickly and energetically enough on toxic pollutants, and the opinion is widely held that acid rain problems — which involve long-range transport of pollutants — cannot be solved within the framework of a system that relies almost exclusively on states in enforcing rules compliance.

Groups supporting stronger clean air legislation are much less advanced with their work than are the industrial associations. Many observers attribute the environmentalists' slow start to their shortage of money, the loss of several leading clean air experts to the Carter administration[16] and to their preoccupation with the issues that were high on the legislative agenda in 1979-80, such as toxic dumping, Alaska lands, and nuclear regulation. However that may be, supporters of clean air legislation will need all the help they can get.

One source of support may be federal, state and local environmental officials. According to S. William Becker, who represents the Association of Local Air Pollution Control Officials (ALAPCO) and the State and Territorial Air Pollution Program Administrators (STAPPA) in Washington, D.C., local officials would like to have more discretion in implementing federal rules and they agree with business groups that federal regulation needs to be made more fast and efficient. But they also think "a lot of these problems are administrative items that may be ironed out administratively without a complete revamping of the Clean Air Act."[17]

Labor's position seems to be divided. The United Steel Workers of America, for example, has not accepted the argument that air regulations are largely responsible for the industry's problems, according to Jack Sheehan, a USW official who is serving on the National Commission on Air Quality. "Our people are constantly pushed with this environmental blackmail, but we have resisted that and have not joined in the general attack on EPA," he said in an interview Oct. 29. The United Auto Workers union, on the other hand, has tended to support relaxation of emission standards, and the United Mine Workers has been an important force opposing strict anti-sulfur regulations. The AFL-CIO's construction unions are participants in NEDA's drive to relax clean air standards.

As for the general public, in a recent poll commissioned by the Council for Environmental Quality, only 20 percent of the people sampled agreed that "we must relax environmen-

---

[15] Interview, Oct. 27, 1980.
[16] For example, CEQ Chairman Gus Speth and David Hawkins, EPA assistant administrator for air, noise and radiation, both worked for the Natural Resources Defense Council in Washington, D.C., before taking jobs with the Carter administration.
[17] Interview, Oct. 29, 1980.

tal standards in order to achieve economic growth," and 42 percent thought environmental problems "so important . . . that continuing improvement must be made regardless of cost." But only 27 percent agreed that economic growth should be sacrificed to protect the environment, compared to 58 percent in 1978.[18]

Balance of Power in the 97th Congress

Last June, EPA Administrator Costle expressed anxiety that the Clean Air Act might be "gutted" in 1981.[19] For one thing, he said, the "inherent complexities of air pollution control make it easy for an opponent to propose language changes which — seemingly innocuous on their face — in fact weaken the law to a serious degree." Still more serious, he said, "is the fact that at no time since the late 1800s . . . have private interests had such influence in Congress as they do today. In 1974, there were 608 political action committees organized to channel funds to candidates. . . . By December 1979 . . . the number of such committees had jumped threefold, to nearly 2,000. . . . Labor union representation had held relatively stable, at 240; trade associations had grown to 512 from 38; corporate committees, by contrast, have soared from 89 to 979."[20]

As a result of the Reagan landslide, Costle soon will be out of a job, and whatever the chances were last June that clean air legislation would be gutted, they now are much higher. In the House, where the Democrats remain in the majority, but by a significantly narrower margin, there is talk of re-organizing the Commerce Committee to reduce the power of Rep. Henry Waxman, D-Calif., chairman of the Health Sub-committee, which has jurisdiction over clean air. Waxman is considered a staunch supporter of clean air. But he is not considered as effective and enthusiastic as was his immediate predecessor as chairman, Rep. Paul G. Rogers, D-Fla., a prin-cipal author of the 1970 Clean Air Act.

Waxman will be under pressure from Rep. Dave Stockman of Michigan, the ranking Republican on the subcommittee. Stockman, a member of the National Commission on Air Qual-ity, "has voiced serious concerns over the fundamental struc-tures of the Clean Air Act" and "can be expected to be a vocal and effective critic of some of the provisions most often criticized by the business community," according to Morris A. Ward, the commission's public affairs director.[21] At the

[18] The poll was conducted by Robert Cameron Mitchell of Resources for the Future in collaboration with the Roper Organization and Cantril Research Inc., and was released by CEQ on Oct. 9, 1980.

[19] Speech to the Air Pollution Control Association, Montreal, Canada, June 23, 1980.

[20] According to the Federal Election Commission, corporate political action committees numbered about 1,100, as of July 1, 1980, and labor PACs about 250.

[21] Speech to an EPA-sponsored meeting of federal, state and local public information officers, Oct. 7, 1980.

same time, Rep. John D. Dingell, D-Mich., a champion of
auto industry interests, will succeed Rep. Harley O. Staggers,
D-W.Va., as chairman of the Commerce Committee. Dingell
fought aggressively in 1976 and 1977 to weaken the auto pollution standards in the Clear Air Act extension.

In the Senate, ironically, committee changes may add up
to a net gain for environmentalists, despite the shift from a
Democratic to a Republican majority. The Energy and Natural
Resources Committee will be headed by Sen. James A. Mc-
Clure, R-Idaho. His predecessor, Henry M. Jackson, D-Wash.
— an ardent advocate of synfuels and an energy mobilization
board — was no favorite of environmentalists. McClure got
a League of Conservation Voters (LCV) rating of 6 for 1979-
80; Jackson got 33.

Chairmanship of the Environmental and Public Works
Committee will go to Sen. Robert T. Stafford, R-Vt., whose
LCV rating was 71, from Sen. Jennings Randolph, D-W.Va.,
a spokesman for coal interests whose LCV rating was 49. And
the chairmanship of the important subcommittee on environmental pollution, where former Sen. Edmund G. Muskie
of Maine took the lead in writing much of the important environmental legislation of the 1970s, will go to Sen. John H.
Chafee, R-R.I., whose LCV rating was 87.[22]

While Stafford and Chafee are well regarded among environmentalists, like Waxman, they may see their powers reduced
in reorganization plans that are being discussed among Republicans in the halls of Congress. In any event, there is general
agreement that the 97th Congress will be more receptive to
arguments for relaxation of government regulations in general
and clean air rules in particular.

Assessment of the Seventies

SIGNIFICANT improvements in the nation's air quality were
not achieved until the late 1970s. As late as May 31, 1975,
the original deadline for compliance with the 1970 Clean Air
Act, pollution levels were higher than specified in the act in
two out of every three air quality regions.[23] By 1979, however,
the Council on Environmental Quality was reporting on the
basis of combined data from 25 metropolitan areas that the
"number of unhealthful days had declined by 15 percent be-

[22] Had the Democrats retained their majority, the chairmanship might have gone to
Sen. Lloyd Bentsen, D-Texas, a spokesman for oil interests.
[23] See "Pollution Control: Costs and Benefits," *E.R.R.*, 1976 Vol. I, pp. 158-161, and
"Auto Emission Controls," *E.R.R.*, 1973 Vol. I, pp. 289-312.

34

Emissions of Major Pollutants, 1970-1977

(millions of metric tons)

Year	Suspended Particles	Sulfur Oxides	Nitrogen Oxides	Hydro-carbons	Carbon Monoxide	Total
1970	22.2	29.8	19.6	29.5	102.2	203.3
1971	20.9	28.3	20.2	29.1	102.5	201.0
1972	19.6	29.6	21.6	29.6	103.8	204.2
1973	19.2	30.2	22.3	29.7	103.5	204.9
1974	17.0	28.4	21.7	28.6	99.7	195.4
1975	13.7	26.1	21.0	26.9	96.9	184.6
1976	13.2	27.2	22.8	28.7	102.9	193.8
1977	12.4	27.4	23.1	28.3	102.7	193.9

Source: Environmental Protection Agency.

tween 1974 and 1977 while the number of very unhealthful days declined 32 percent." The CEQ attributed the decrease mainly to a reduction of auto pollution. Taking data from about 50 of the most polluted counties in the country, the CEQ found that "violations of ambient air quality standards generally either stayed constant or decreased between 1974 and 1977. The greatest improvements were made in reducing violations of the carbon monoxide and sulfur dioxide standards."

Despite the improvements, the council stressed that air pollution was still a problem. "In 1977, the air in two of the 41 urban areas for which reliable data were available still registered in the 'unhealthful' range for more than two-thirds of the days of the year," the council said. "These two, the New York and Los Angeles urban areas, together contain almost 8 percent of the nation's population. Only 16 of the 41 urban areas had 'unhealthful' readings for fewer than 10 percent of the days during the year. . . . The pollutants that most frequently drove index readings into the 'unhealthful' range in the 41 urban areas were carbon monoxide and photochemical oxidents (ozone)."[24]

Ambient air levels for one pollutant, nitrogen dioxide, showed little change during the years 1974-77. But violations of the standards for most of the other "criteria" pollutants — the pollutants for which EPA sets national air quality standards — decreased significantly in at least some areas.[25] Violations of ozone standards generally dropped in the western parts of

---

[24] Council on Environmental Quality, "Environmental Quality - 1979," p. 17. The author of the chapter on air quality in the 1980 CEQ annual report said that figures for 1978 showed continued improvement but also persistent bad days in some metropolitan areas. The 1980 report will contain for the first time data on ambient concentrations of pollutants, as opposed to days in violation of ambient air standards.

[25] EPA standards for particulates, sulfur dioxide, carbon monoxide, hydrocarbons and nitrogen dioxide were set in 1971. The standard for ozone was revised in 1979. A standard for lead was added in 1978.

the United States, but not in the eastern and central parts. Despite improvements, the Los Angeles area continued to suffer more smog violations than any other part of the country. Carbon monoxide levels improved markedly almost everywhere, but most of all in the East, while levels of suspended particulates displayed no strong regional trends. Sulfur dioxide levels generally were not severe except in areas where smelters are located.

Altogether ozone violations decreased 24 percent between 1974 and 1977, carbon monoxide violations, 43 percent; sulfur dioxide, 54 percent; and particulates, 2 percent. Even so, EPA statistics indicate that the total quantity of primary pollutant emissions dropped by less than 10 million metric tons between 1970 and 1977 *(see box, p. 32)*. With the total coming to 193.9 million metric tons in 1977, there was nearly a ton of pollutants for every person in the United States.

Emission Standards Established by EPA

In addition to setting and revising standards for criteria pollutants, EPA has established emission limits for stationary sources of pollution and for hazardous air pollutants. Since 1971, the agency has promulgated "new source performance standards" on an ongoing basis; some 30 such standards cover a variety of industrial processes, municipal incinerators, foundaries, etc. Of these, the most important is the standard for coal-fired power plants, which was revised in May 1979, as mandated in the 1977 Clean Air Amendments. The revised standard required 70-90 percent of the sulfur to be removed from coal stack emissions, depending on the coal's sulfur content — a compromise between high-sulfur and low-sulfur coal states. Another important performance standard, the one for coal-fired industrial boilers, is scheduled for promulgation next year.

In 1973, EPA issued standards for three hazardous substances — asbestos, beryllium and mercury. Standards for vinyl chloride, polyvinyl chloride and benzene were issued subsequently. The agency currently is developing a standard for arsenic, to be issued next spring, and a proposal for a general policy on carcinogenic air pollutants was issued in October 1979. Under the proposed policy, when (1) a substance is determined to be a clear carcinogen; (2) that judgment holds up under review; and (3) a population is clearly at risk, then regulations will be issued based on best available technology. Thereupon an assessment will be made of what it would cost to develop technology that would clean up the substance altogether.[26]

---

[26] Many hazardous substances are dangerous only when exposure exceeds a certain threshold, and EPA therefore sets a standard that prevents that threshold from being crossed. But with carcinogens there is no safe level of exposure — hence the procedure proposed in 1979.

Auto Waivers: Model Years 1981-82*

	Carbon Monoxide		Nitrogen Oxides**	
	Requests	Granted	Requests	Granted
Domestic***	42	15	16	1
Foreign	27	6	9	11

*Some waivers granted are for one year, some for two. Among the requests not granted, a few cases are still pending, but most were denied.
**All requests were for diesel cars except for one from American Motors Corporation, which was granted.
***General Motors filed 28 requests; Ford, 3; Chrysler, 9; AMC, 2. GM was granted 4; Ford, 3; Chrysler, 6; AMC, 2.

Many of EPA's decisions on standards have been controversial either because industries considered them too onerous, or because environmentalists thought them too lax, or both. For example, when the agency relaxed the ozone standard in January 1979, questions were raised as to whether it had violated its mandate not to take the costs of compliance into account when setting standards. The diesel emission standards which the agency set for cars and trucks last February impressed some environmentalists as a concession to the U.S. auto industry. But other environmentalists — concerned about U.S. dependence on oil from the volatile Middle East — thought that the standard was too tight and would hamper the development of highly fuel efficient diesel cars.[27]

Controversy Over Waivers, State Plans

The 1977 Clean Air Amendments gave EPA the authority to grant waivers covering carbon monoxide and nitrogen oxide emissions for 1980 and 1981 cars.[28] Newspaper reports of occasional waivers being granted have tended to create the impression that the agency has been liberal with the industry. In fact, the agency has rejected most requests, and the waivers it has granted cover only about 28 percent of the vehicles scheduled for sale in 1981 (see box, above).

Another equally touchy set of decisions that EPA officials have been responsible for making during the last year concerns the revised State Implementation Plans (SIPs), which were to have been approved by July 1, 1979, under the 1977 amendments. Many states failed to meet the deadline; as of October 1980, 12 of the 52 states and territories still had not submitted

---

[27] See Dick Kirschten, "EPA's Ozone Standard Faces a Hazy Future," *National Journal,* Dec. 16, 1978, pp. 2015-2019, and the letter from Stephen J. Gage of EPA's Office of Research and Development to *Science* magazine, Feb. 23, 1979, pp. 22-23.
[28] Between 1975 and 1977 auto manufacturers obtained several extensions on emission deadlines, the net effect of which was to shift the final dates for compliance by a total of five years. The 1977 amendments tightened 1980-1981 standards for hydrocarbons, carbon monoxide and nitrogen oxides, but authorized EPA to grant waivers for carbon monoxide and nitrogen oxides.

complete plans. Of the 40 complete plans that were submitted, EPA had approved 18 in full and 15 in part, and on seven it had taken no final action.[29] EPA had taken final action on five out of the 11 partial plans submitted, and it gave Hawaii extra time to submit a plan because of the state's uniquely limited air quality problems.

Many state and local officials have complained, along with industry representatives, about EPA's slowness in acting on plans. But EPA members say that the agency has been slow mainly because it has been "bending over backwards" not to disapprove plans formally — an action that would mean costly delays in getting permits for new plants and cut-offs of federal highway and sewage funds. Agency officials and other environmentalists fear that imposition of such severe sanctions would cause a backlash against clean air legislation.

Prospects for the Future

CLEANING the air presents ever-changing regulatory problems to which there will never be any permanent solutions. As consumption habits, lifestyles and industrial processes are modified, the sources of pollution change as well, and regulators struggle to keep up.

As energy prices skyrocketed in the 1970s, to take just one example, it became fashionable and economical for Americans living in New England, the northern midwestern states, the Northwest and even the Southeast to heat their homes with wood. More than one-third of the households in New England now burn wood for winter heating, and in 1979 roughly 1.5 million wood-burning stoves were sold nationwide. Although burning wood strikes many people as a happy and wholesome activity, wood combustion emits annoying particulates that aggravate respiratory ailments. Even more serious, wood combustion produces polycyclic organic materials ("POMs"), which are known carcinogens. Some communities already have passed ordinances that limit installation of fireplaces in new buildings.[30]

If wood burning continues to grow in popularity, federal action on wood emissions eventually may be necessary. Other changes in customs may present similar problems. In the immediate future, however, the country's greatest air quality prob-

---

[29] Approval generally was given subject to certain conditions, and minor aspects of some fully approved plans still had to be revised.
[30] See Michael Harris, "King Coal and Wood Heat," *New Hampshire Times,* fall 1980 special issue, and an article by Robert Deis in the (forthcoming) December issue of *Environmental Action.*

lems will continue to arise from auto use and from industrial sources of pollution.

Stationary, Mobile Sources of Pollution

Industrial facilities and combustion account for nearly all sulfur oxide emissions, over 80 percent of particulate emissions and over half of nitrogen oxide emissions *(See box, p. 40)*. Because of the problems facing many of the nation's largest industries, there may be growing pressure to relax air regulations affecting industries and even to junk the State Implementation Plans (SIP) prepared with so much fuss during the past decade.

William Pedersen, a deputy general counsel with EPA, said in a paper recently distributed to agency officials that the clean air law "lacks any clearly defined mechanism for establishing with precision the sum total of requirements a given source must obey." He described the SIP process as overly cumbersome because it "requires affirmative action by at least

Major Sources of Air Pollutants

	Suspended Particles	Sulfur Oxides	Hydro-carbons	Nitrogen Oxides	Carbon Monoxide
Transpor-tation	9%	3%	41%	40%	83%
Combustion	39%	82%	5%	56%	1%
Industrial Processes	43%	15%	36%	4%	8%
Solid Waste	3%	—	2%	—	3%
Miscella-neous	6%	—	16%	—	5%

Source: Environmental Protection Agency.

two levels of government." Pedersen suggested scrapping most of the SIP process in favor of a simpler permitting system. Many regulatory officials agree that the procedures have been awkward, but some seem to think that the process of forcing all relevant interests to collaborate in preparing a clean air plan is valuable. Mark Pisano of the Southern California Association of Governments, which prepared the transportation parts of the clean air plan for the Los Angeles region, reports that the "full head of steam" that local organizations built up during preparation of the plan tended to dissipate because EPA took so long evaluating the plan. He went on to say that preparation of the plan otherwise represented a valuable experience for all involved.[31]

EPA took its time with the California plan in large part because of the state legislature's refusal to enact a vehicle inspection and maintenance program, as required by the 1977 Clean Air Amendments. Generally the agency has avoided imposing sanctions in connection with SIP approvals, but it has insisted — as it must under the law — that states getting extensions on compliance deadlines implement inspection programs for cars. This year EPA embargoed new construction permits in Colorado for this reason, and after just two days the state legislature enacted an inspection program. California is likely to be the next state to see sanctions imposed.

Some environmentalists have urged EPA to push states much harder to promote mass transit and adopt regional land-use planning as means of reducing auto use. The incoming Republican administration is likely to be even less receptive to such ideas than was the Carter administration. If we now are entering a period of fiscal austerity and government policy based on free market economics, as the Republicans have promised, market forces may be the best hope for reduced auto emissions

[31] Interview, Nov. 6, 1980.

Health Effects of Major Pollutants

The Environmental Protection Agency has responsibility for determining what kinds of air pollutants are hazardous to public health and welfare and setting standards for each. EPA standards have been set for the following seven pollutants:

Sulfur dioxide. This corrosive and poisonous gas is associated with coughs, colds, asthma and bronchitis and can aggravate heart disorders. Together with nitrogen dioxide, sulfur dioxide can go through chemical transformations in the air to form acid rain, which can kill fish and retard growth of vegetation.

Nitrogen dioxide. A poisonous and highly reactive gas, nitrogen dioxide can be fatal at very high concentrations. At lower levels, it can reduce resistance to respiratory diseases such as bronchitis and pneumonia. Still more important, it reacts with hydrocarbons in sunlit air to form ozone, the principal constituent of smog.

Ozone. A pungent smelling, faintly bluish gas, ozone is a poisonous form of pure oxygen. It irritates the mucous membranes of the respiratory system, causing choking and coughing, and aggravating respiratory diseases.

Carbon monoxide. This colorless, odorless gas replaces oxygen in red blood cells, reducing the amount of oxygen that reaches cells in the body. Sustained exposure to high levels affects the brain initially, impairing perception and thinking, slowing reflexes, weakening judgment and inducing drowsiness. Eventually the heart is affected as well. At very high levels of exposure, a person can die from heart failure or asphyxiation. Other symptoms of exposure to carbon monoxide include headaches, dizziness, nausea and difficulty in breathing.

Particulates. Generally thought of as dust, soot and smoke, particulates can include many kinds of solid and liquid substances, some of them highly toxic. The health hazards caused by particulates can be physical, resulting from the clogging of the lung sacs by fine particles, or chemical. Particulates passing to vital organs via the lungs and bloodstream can react adversely with substances in the body. The presence of particulates in conjunction with sulfur oxides can severely aggravate respiratory diseases.

Lead. Roughly 90 percent of airborne lead comes from auto emissions. Lead smelting and processing industries also are significant sources. Lead concentrates in bone and soft body tissues. Its most pronounced effects are on the blood-forming, nervous and kidney systems. Young children are especially susceptible to lead poisoning.

Hydrocarbons. Primarily a product of automobile fuel combustion, hydrocarbons are unburned fuels in gaseous or vapor form. At the levels generally prevailing in the air, hydrocarbons may have no direct effect on human health. In a confined space, of course, they could cause asphyxiation by displacing the air. A serious problem with hydrocarbons stems from the oxidants they help to form by reacting with nitrogen oxides in sunlight.

in the years to come. To the extent Americans continue to buy smaller, more fuel-efficient cars, emissions will be cut roughly in proportion to the drop in gasoline consumption. Some of the new automobile engine technologies under development promise to have lower emission rates.[32]

Costs and Benefits of Cleaning the Air

The general philosophy of the Reagan administration likely will be to subject all environmental regulations to rigorous cost-benefit analysis. In this approach, which the business community generally favors, the government makes public policy decisions the same way a company or a consumer would make a decision about what to buy. That is to say, the government tries very hard not to pay more for anything than it is worth. But in matters of public policy, as in questions of personal consumption, it often is a lot easier to tell what something costs than it is to determine what one is going to get out of owning it. Once you have bought a product, you may be disappointed with it. On the other hand, if you don't buy it, you may not appreciate just how useful or pleasurable it could be.

"We believe that it is imperative that environmental laws and regulations be reviewed, and where necessary, reformed to ensure that the benefits achieved justify the costs imposed. . . ."

Republican Party Platform
adopted July 15, 1980

The Council on Environmental Quality has estimated that total public and private expenditures on air pollution control came to $19.3 billion in 1978 — close to half of the nation's spending on pollution abatement. The expenditures on air pollution control that resulted from federal legislation were estimated at $16.6 billion.[33] A study commissioned by CEQ estimated the benefits of air pollution control, including improved public health, reduced cleaning expenses, better vegetation, less damage to materials and higher property values, at $21.4 billion in 1978. But the study said that the true benefits in 1978 could have been as low as $4.6 million or as high

---

[32] See "Auto Research and Regulation," *E.R.R.*, 1979 Vol. I, pp. 145-164.
[33] "Environmental Quality - 1979," p. 666.

Keeping Clean Air Clean

The 1977 Clean Air Amendments strengthened efforts to maintain air quality in regions where the air already is clean. Under the law, there cannot be any "significant deterioration" of air quality in such regions. The law specifies how sulfur oxides and particulates *(see box, p. 41)* will be regulated in clean-air regions, and anticipates later regulation of other pollutants.

Three kinds of clean-air regions are defined. Class I includes all national parks and wilderness areas and may include further areas named by the states to remain unsullied. No significant additional sulfur or particulate sources are permitted in Class I regions.

Class II areas can have some industrial development, up to specified levels. Class III areas can have about twice as much pollution from additional sources, sometimes up to the minimum federal standards.

as $51.2 billion, and it concluded that "the estimation of certain kinds of environmental benefits is still in need of much additional refinement."[34]

Industry groups have not accepted current estimates of the benefits resulting from air quality control, and a lot of figures will be bandied about in the coming debate over clean air legislation. In the end, the future of air pollution regulations may well depend on how people feel about the air they breathe and on whether they are willing to make sacrifices to make it cleaner, rather than on elaborate cost-benefit analysis.

---

[34] *The Benefits of Air and Water Pollution Controls: A Review and Synthesis of Recent Estimates* (1979), executive summary.

Selected Bibliography

Books

Denison, Edward F., *Accounting for Slower Economic Growth: The United States in the 1970s,* The Brookings Institution, 1978.

Weidenbaum, Murray L., *Business, Government and the Public,* Prentice-Hall, 1977.

——*The Cost of Federal Regulation of Economic Activity,* American Enterprise Institute, 1978.

Articles

Air and Water Pollution Report, selected issues.

Baldwin, Deborah and Gail Robinson, "Fear and Loathing in the Cower Tower: EPA - 10 Years After," *Environmental Action,* June 1980.

Carter, Luther J., "Uncontrolled SO_2 Emissions Bring Acid Rain," *Science,* June 15, 1979.

Cleveland, William S. and T. E. Graedel, "Photochemical Air Pollution in the Northeast United States," *Science,* June 22, 1979.

Environmental Reporter (published by the Bureau of National Affairs), selected issues.

Inside EPA, selected issues.

Johnson, Greg, "How Clean Is Clean Air?" *Industry Week,* Sept. 15, 1980.

Kirschten, Dick, "EPA's Ozone Standard Faces a Hazy Future," *National Journal,* Dec. 16, 1978.

Koch, Kathy, "Philosophical Split Divides Candidates on Environment," *Congressional Quarterly Weekly Report,* Oct. 18, 1980.

——and Ann Pelham, "Future of Coal," *Congressional Quarterly Weekly Report,* May 31, 1980.

Mosher, Lawrence, "Big Steel Says It Can't Afford to Make the Nation's Air Pure," *National Journal,* July 5, 1980.

Reports and Studies

Council on Environmental Quality, "Environmental Quality — 1979," 10th annual report, 1979.

Editorial Research Reports: "Acid Rain," 1980 Vol. I, p. 445; "Closing the Environmental Decade," 1979 Vol. II, p. 821; "Auto Research and Regulation," 1979 Vol. I, p. 145; "Auto Emission Controls," 1973 Vol. I, p. 289.

Environmental Protection Agency, "Cleaning the Air," OPA 48/8, June 1979.

——"The Cost of Clean Air and Water," EPA 230/3-79-001, August 1979.

Freeman, A. Myrick, "The Benefits of Air and Water Pollution Control," prepared for the Council on Environmental Quality, December 1979.

League of Conservation Voters, "The Presidential Candidates," 1980.

PESTICIDE CONTROVERSIES

by

Tom Arrandale

Apr. 30
1 9 8 2

PESTICIDE CONTROVERSIES

S INCE men first tilled the earth, farmers have fought endless battles with pests that prey on crops and livestock. For 40 years, the agricultural industry has waged all-out war on insects, disease, worms and weeds with modern-day chemical weapons. But powerful pesticides, once hailed as miracles of science, have spread mixed blessings on the fields.

Agricultural pests still consume at least one-third of the food crops that the world grows each year. Synthetic chemical pesticides, while helping farmers double crop yields, have also bred resistant insects and set new pests loose by killing their natural enemies. Sprayed indiscriminately across the fields by helicopters or low-flying "crop dusters," lethal compounds have killed wildlife, contaminated soil and streams, and built up in human tissues.

Americans first became aware of the possible hazards of widespread pesticide use with the publication in 1962 of *Silent Spring* by Rachel Carson. In the book, which became a national best-seller, Carson argued that many pesticides in use on farms and timberlands had unknown and cumulative toxic effects. Because so little was known about the effects of these chemicals, Carson said, their use should be curtailed.

The federal government in the 1970s banned most uses of DDT (dichlorodiphenyl trichloroethane) and other potent chemicals that threatened human health and environmental safety. Despite stricter government regulations, pesticide spraying doubled over the last two decades as farmers turned to new chemical compounds to protect their harvests and make their fields more productive. U.S. farmers now apply about 700 million pounds of insecticides, herbicides and fungicides a year, at a cost of around $2 billion.

Despite such weapons, pests still plague the world's most productive agricultural country. In developing lands, where the specter of famine still looms, the fight against pests may be more desperate. "Neither the hungry nor the affluent can continue to pay this price, which is to receive only part of their daily bread," wrote William R. Furtick, former chief of the United Nations Food and Agriculture Organization.[1]

---

[1] William R. Furtick, "Uncontrolled Pests or Adequate Food?" in D. L. Gunn and J. G. R. Stevens, ed., *Pesticides and Human Welfare* (1976), p. 3.

Defining Pesticides

Pesticide is a general term for any substance or mixture of substances intended for preventing, destroying, repelling, or mitigating any pest, including insects, rodents, fungi or weeds. The Environmental Protection Agency (EPA) has registered between 35,000 and 40,000 pesticide products, all made from one or more of about 600 basic chemical compounds. EPA also has registered about 1,200 active pesticide ingredients. There are three major types of synthetic pesticides, classified by chemical components:

● Chlorinated hydrocarbons, or organochlorines, are "hard" pesticides that break down chemically quite slowly and can remain in the environment for long periods. They include DDT, DDD, DDE, Dieldrin, chlordane, toxaphene, aldrin, endrin, helptachlor and lindane.

● Organic phosphates, or organophosphates are highly toxic to humans but are not persistent in the environment. They include parathion, malathion, chlarethion, thimet, phosdrin, methylparathion and trichlorphone.

● Carbamates are compounds that have low toxicity to humans.

Source: Congressional Quarterly Inc., *Environment and Health* (1981), p. 82.

From the Biblical locust plagues to California's recent "Medfly" invasion,[2] agricultural pests have posed threats to food supplies. In agrarian and industrial societies alike, on peasants' plots and mechanized agribusiness farms, huge amounts of food are lost before ever reaching the table. A 1977 National Academy of Sciences study estimated that pests cost the world about 35 percent of its potential food production.[3]

Pests afflict all the world's major crops, infest forests and attack horses, sheep and cattle. Along with the celebrated Medfly, common pests go by such colorful names as the gypsy moth, boll weevil, grasshopper, Hessian fly, blights and rusts, wild oats and wild buckwheat. They include insects, weeds, worms, bacteria, fungi, rodents and larger mammals that nibble crops or prey on domestic livestock.

Since World War II, farmers have relied on synthetic chemical pesticides as their principal defense against pest losses. Pesticide spraying has grown tenfold since 1945 — and more than doubled since *Silent Spring* was published in 1962. More than 1,200 basic ingredients now are labeled for pesticide use, and 35,000 formulations have been registered. Farmers use a

[2] California's fruit and vegetable crops were threatened by a Mediterranean fruit fly infestation that started in spring 1980. Aerial pesticide spraying to control the problem set off a storm of protest by environmentalists and residents of the San Francisco suburbs *(see p. 49)*.

[3] National Research Council, Commission on International Relations, National Academy of Sciences, "Supporting Papers: World Food and Nutrition Study," 1977, p. 102.

relatively small number, depending on 20 insecticides to combat insects, 17 herbicides to keep down weeds and six fungicides to prevent plant diseases.[4]

Pesticides have helped farmers around the world harvest larger crops and send more food to market. Norman E. Borlaug, a crop researcher who was awarded the 1970 Nobel Peace Prize for his work in launching the "green revolution" in Asia, contended in 1972 that banning chemical pesticides would cut crop yields in half and raise food prices four or five times.[5] The congressional Office of Technology Assessment (OTA) in 1979 concluded that without pesticides — or equally effective alternative measures — grain prices would jump 60 percent and commercial producers of lettuce, apples, potatoes and strawberries would suffer intolerable losses.[6]

Pest losses remain high, however, even with widespread spraying. Insect damage has nearly doubled since 1945, and herbicides at best have slightly curtailed weed problems. At the same time, many people worry that campaigns to curb a few unwanted species could endanger the entire fabric of life on earth. Environmentalists now demand, in Rachel Carson's words, that "the methods employed [to control pests] must be such that they do not destroy us along with the insects."[7]

Since 1970, when regulation was transferred from the U.S. Agriculture Department to the newly created Environmental Protection Agency (EPA), the federal government has tightened controls over the manufacturing, distribution and use of pesticides *(see p. 51).* Even so, fears persist that pesticides now being sprayed will eventually turn out to be damaging to wildlife and humans. "In the past we willingly accepted claims that pesticides had no long-term effect on humans," Douglas M. Costle, EPA administrator under President Carter, has commented. "Neither EPA nor the industry is in a position to make such reassurances honestly."[8]

Medfly Spraying, Other Controversies

Such doubts were apparent in several recent pest control controversies. In California, farmers and state officials are watching carefully for any reinvasion by Mediterranean fruit flies, which threatened the state's fruit and vegetable crops in

[4] U.S. Congress, Office of Technology Assessment (OTA), "Pest Management Strategies" in Crop Protection," 1979, p. 19.
[5] Norman E. Borlaug, "Mankind and Civilization at Another Crossroads," *BioScience,* 22: 41-44, 1972. See also "Green Revolution," *E.R.R.,* 1970 Vol. I, pp. 219-238.
[6] Office of Technology Assessment, *op. cit.,* pp. 78-79.
[7] Rachel Carson, *Silent Spring* (1962), p. 9
[8] Quoted by Allen A. Boraiko, "The Pesticide Dilemma," *National Geographic,* February 1980, p. 150.

1980 and 1981. Over vehement local objections, California Gov. Edmund G. (Jerry) Brown Jr. authorized aerial spraying over heavily populated suburbs last July to keep the hardy insects from spreading from backyard fruit trees into the state's rich agricultural Central Valley.

No Medflies have been sighted in the state since Nov. 20, 1981,[9] but California officials are not taking any chances. In mid-April they resumed weekly sprayings of the pesticide malathion over 166.6 square miles, primarily in the northern part of the state. The sprayings will be phased out in mid-June if no new flies or larvae are found.

Brown approved aerial spraying last year only after U.S. Secretary of Agriculture John Block threatened to quarantine California produce to keep the Medfly from spreading. Brown earlier had tried to fight the pests by ordering residents to destroy infested fruits and vegetables and by spraying from the ground. Brown gave in despite public fears that malathion, a non-persistent but highly toxic organic phosphate, would endanger residents of the 1,486-square-mile area where aerial spraying was conducted in 1981.

Gov. Brown

The dispute sparked the sharpest pest control conflict yet between urban and agricultural interests. Some critics, including Stanford University biologist Paul Ehrlich, said that other methods could have kept the Medflies under control without aerial spraying. But Dick Jackson, deputy director of a joint state and federal Medfly project, argued that the spraying "opened the door to a sensible use of pesticides." In California, Jackson insisted, "we've proven that we haven't even made anybody sick and have done a hell of a lot for our credibility." [10]

But public concern over pesticide spraying remains high. Citizens in New England and New York metropolitan areas have objected to chemical sprayings to protect trees against gypsy moth caterpillars, which attack more than 500 plant species. California farm workers have sued farmers and pesticide manufacturers, complaining that picking fruits and vegetables in recently sprayed fields has permanently damaged their health.

---

[9] State officials first spotted Medflies in California's Santa Clara Valley in June 1980.
[10] Quoted by John Walsh, "Medfly Continues to Bug California," *Science,* Dec. 11, 1981, p. 1222. See also Mary Barnett and Janet Marinelli, "Medfly Madness," *Environmental Action,* September 1981, pp. 10-14.

Last fall, state and federal wildlife officials in the West debated canceling hunting seasons after dangerous levels of the acutely toxic pesticide endrin were found in ducks, geese and other game birds in Montana. The birds, which apparently had fed on wheat and other grains sprayed with the pesticide, contained endrin traces that were potentially hazardous for persons who shot and ate the fowl. Environmentalists from Massachusetts to Oregon have blamed increasing cancer rates and other health problems on picloram, a herbicide that the U.S. Forest Service and timber companies use to clear hardwoods from pine forests and that railroads and power companies spray to keep rights-of-way free of weeds.[11]

The Reagan administration rekindled another pest control debate last January by moving to allow use of chemical toxicants to control coyotes on federal rangelands in Western states *(see p. 59).* President Nixon, responding to environmentalists' outcries, in 1972 banned use of those poisons, including Compound 1080 (sodium monofluoroacetate), in predator control programs on federally owned lands. EPA subsequently clamped severe limits on state and private use of Compound 1080, strychnine and other toxicants as baits to kill coyotes. Environmentalists argued that the toxicants killed other wildlife, including endangered species, that ate the baits or fed on the carcasses of coyotes.

Government Regulations and Controls

U.S. pesticide regulation dates from early in the 20th century. Responding to pressure from farm organizations and the U.S. Department of Agriculture (USDA), Congress in 1910 set standards for ingredients in Paris green, lead arsenate and other pesticides then being used. In 1947, with new synthetic chemical pesticides coming on the market, Congress enacted the Federal Insecticide, Fungicide and Rodenticide Act (FIFRA) requiring for the first time that all pesticides be registered before going on the market and that packages be labeled with their contents. USDA administered the law, concentrating on making sure that pesticides worked as claimed. Few chemicals were barred from the market.[12]

Responsibility for regulation of pesticides was transferred from the Agriculture Department to the Environmental Protection Agency when it was created in 1970. Congress in 1972 strengthened EPA's regulation and enforcement powers by passing the Federal Environmental Pesticide Control Act,

---

[11] Keith Schneider, "Agent White — It Kills Weeds, Bushes, Trees — and Maybe People," *Inquiry*, March 15, 1981, p. 14.
[12] See National Research Council, National Academy of Sciences, "Regulating Pesticides," 1980.

which empowered the agency to control pesticide manufacturing, distribution and use, to ban hazardous chemicals and impose penalties for improper use. Congress in 1978 adopted legislation to simplify pesticide registration and marketing procedures, allowing EPA to classify and register pesticides by chemical composition rather than product name. In 1980, Congress gave itself authority to veto EPA pesticide rules; both the House and Senate must approve the veto, however.[13]

Environmentalists have demanded tougher EPA pesticide regulation. Farmers and the chemical industry, on the other hand, argue that federal rules have exaggerated pesticide threats and slowed development of improved pesticide compounds. Chemical producers contend that stringent federal and state standards and time-consuming registration procedures discourage development of new insecticides targeted on specific pests.

Congress is now considering legislation to extend and perhaps modify the Federal Insecticide, Fungicide and Rodenticide Act. Pesticide producers are urging the House Agriculture Committee's Subcommittee on Department Operations, Research and Foreign Agriculture to limit public access to industry studies on how various chemical compounds affect human health and the environment. The companies contend that the toxicity studies contain trade secrets. Industry officials also have asked Congress to pre-empt state laws, which sometimes — as in California — are more restrictive than federal regulations. Environmentalists, fearful that pesticide controls will be watered down, want FIFRA extended without change.[14]

Worldwide Pest Problems

FARMERS have contended with pests ever since men first cultivated crops 10,000 or more years ago. The Bible describes several crop and livestock infestations, including the locust plague on Egypt that "covered the face of the whole earth, so that the land was darkened...." [15] Early civilizations lived in fear of plagues that could bring famine upon the land, and more recent infestations at times have changed the course

[13] For background, see Congressional Quarterly Inc., *Environment and Health* (1981), pp. 81-84.
[14] See Francesca Lyman, "Industry to Government: 'Let Us Spray,'" *Environmental Action*, November 1981, p. 16, and Kathy Koch, "House Committee Reviewing Pesticide Law," *Congressional Quarterly Weekly Report*, Feb. 20, 1982, pp. 337-338.
[15] *Exodus* 10:13-15 (Authorized, King James Version).

More than half of a pesticide sprayed from the air drifts off-target.

of history. After a blight destroyed Ireland's potato crop in 1845, a million Irish died and a million and a half more emigrated to America. In 1916-17, U.S. grain farmers lost at least a third of their harvest to wheat rust disease, and the resulting food crisis may have delayed the nation's entrance into World War I.[16]

Developing lands, especially in tropical climates, still are threatened with calamity. But even in industrial countries, where farming has been mechanized, men compete for food with a host of organisms. In many cases, modern agricultural practices have created more problems for farmers and ranchers by encouraging the spread of new pests.

Specialized monocultural farms, growing vast stretches of a single cash crop, have given some pests free rein to spread unchecked from field to neighboring field. The western corn rootworm, for instance, has been expanding its range by 140 miles a year as it moves through North America's Midwest Corn Belt. Some once-harmless organisms, like the Colorado potato beetle, spread quickly across the continent when farmers began planting new crops that the pests thrived on. Some exotic species, like the Medfly, gypsy moth, and Japanese beetle, have prospered in North America after being inadvertently brought from overseas.

Insects and related anthropods — from the housefly to the grasshopper — are perhaps the most common and prolific pests. Throughout the world, about 10,000 species of insect are considered important pests for crops, livestock, stored foods and people. The United States has 150 to 200 insect species that pose serious pest problems.

---

[16] George Borgstrom, *Too Many: The Biological Limitations of Our Earth* (1969).

Weeds are simply unwanted plants that compete with crops for sunlight, water and soil nutrients. More than 30,000 plant species are classified as weeds, and more than 1,800 cause economic losses to agriculture. Plant diseases caused by fungi, worm-like nematodes, viruses and bacteria also take large tolls from crop production. And livestock diseases, parasites and predators kill, maim and weaken domestic horses, sheep and cattle.[17]

A National Academy of Sciences study team reported in 1977 that insects, weeds and plant diseases posed serious threats to all the world's major crops. Pests consumed 20 percent of all important harvests, their report concluded, and ruined 46.4 percent of yearly rice crops, which provide the staple for many nations' diets. Post-harvest losses of stored foods to rodents, insects, fungi and bacteria lifted the total toll on the world's food supplies to more than 40 percent.[18]

Modern Reliance on Chemical Pesticides

Early farmers developed a number of measures through trial and error to limit losses to pests. Around 2,500 B.C., Sumerians used sulfur compounds to control mites and insects. Centuries before Christ, the Chinese developed plant-derived insecticides, adjusted planting times and used natural enemies to keep pests in check. And through the centuries, farmers cultivated the soil by hand, with hoes and eventually horse-drawn plows, to rid the soil of weeds before planting.[19]

During the late 19th and early 20th centuries, public agricultural experiment stations in farming states developed techniques to suppress pests through resistant crop varieties, cultivation practices, and biological control through natural enemies. After the boll weevil spread into Southern cotton fields from Mexico in the late 1800s, farmers fought back by planting varieties that matured earlier in the year, before weevils became numerous. They also destroyed post-harvest crop residues and adjusted harvesting schedules to hold down damage from weevils that bored into cotton plant bolls.

As early as 1865, however, American farmers began using an arsenic compound called Paris green to control the Colorado potato beetle. Kansas farmers applied common salt to kill bindweed in the late 1800s, and wheat farmers introduced copper sulfate to control weeds around the turn of the century.

---

[17] Dale R. Bottrell, "Integrated Pest Management," Council on Environmental Quality, 1979, p. 1.
[18] National Research Council, Commission on International Relations, *op. cit.*, pp. 102-103.
[19] George Ordish, *The Constant Pest* (1976).

Farmers started spraying orchards with lead arsenate in 1892 and dusting crops with calcium arsenate in 1907. After 1886, California citrus trees were fumigated under tarpaulin tents with hydrogen cyanide.[20] Aerial spraying from aircraft expanded pesticide use in the 1920s.

After World War II, the chemical industry marketed more effective synthetic organic pesticides, including the insecticide DDT and the herbicide 2,4-D, which had been developed during wartime.[21] During postwar years, German industry modified chemical warfare agents to produce organic phosphate compounds, including parathion and malathion, for use as pesticides.

At first, synthetic pesticides brought spectacular results in controlling insects in productive farming regions. Herbicides replaced costly hand labor and machine cultivation for controlling weeds in fields, in forests and along highways, railroads and utility lines. Pesticides offered improved pest control to protect the high-yielding wheat, rice, maize and other food grains that Borlaug and other researchers developed for the "green revolution" in developing lands *(see p. 49)*. DDT improved human health in entire countries by controlling pests like the malaria-carrying mosquito.

Unexpected Consequences and Hazards

In the United States, a major industry grew up in postwar decades to develop and sell synthetic pesticides.[22] U.S. production climbed from around 464,000 pounds in 1946 to 1.4 billion pounds in 1977 as pesticides were applied in agriculture, forests, industry and households. But by 1962, when *Silent Spring* sounded a public alarm, unexpected consequences were already tarnishing the once-bright promise of effective pest control.

After prolonged exposure to particular pesticides, pest populations began to develop genetic resistance. As susceptible insects were killed off, hardier survivors mated to produce offspring that inherited immunity. Over the 30 years after synthetic chemicals were introduced, more than 300 species of insects, mites and ticks evolved strains that were resistant to one or more pesticides. The corn rootworm, tobacco budworm and the common housefly now survive pesticides that once were fatal.

---

[20] A. W. A. Brown, *Ecology of Pesticides* (1978), pp. 1-10.

[21] DDT, a synthetic organochlorine, was first formulated in 1874, but its power to kill insects was not discovered until 1939. The U.S. Army classified DDT "top secret" during World War II, and the Allies used it to protect their troops against insect-borne diseases that inflicted widespread casualties among German forces.

[22] More than 80 U.S. companies produce active ingredients for pesticides, and as many as 1,800 firms manufacture and package pesticide dusts, powders, concentrates and aerosols. Spending on pesticides surpassed $1.9 billion in 1976. See U.S. Council on Environmental Quality, "Integrated Pest Management," 1979, p. 7.

Agent Orange

During the Vietnam War, the U.S. Army used Agent Orange — a combination of two herbicides, 2,4,5-T and 2,4-D — to defoliate dense jungles concealing enemy forces. Many U.S. veterans later blamed exposure to Agent Orange for a variety of health disorders, including cancer, liver damage, psychological and neurological symptoms, miscarriages, stillbirths and birth defects in their children.

The component in Agent Orange that is suspected of causing health problems, TCDD, is a contaminant of 2,4,5-T — that is, a substance inadvertently created in varying amounts in the manufacturing process. TCDD is the most toxic of approximately 75 chemical compounds known as dioxins.

The Defense Department ended its Agent Orange spraying in Vietnam in 1970. In May 1970 the Agriculture Department moved to end the use of 2,4,5-T products on food crops and near homes, recreation sites and other areas. In 1972 the ban on 2,4,5-T products was successfully challenged in court by Dow Chemical Co.

The Environmental Protection Agency, which had taken over most of the Agriculture Department's regulatory responsibilities for agricultural chemicals, resumed ban proceedings again the following year, but abandoned the process and turned to studies instead. In 1979 EPA suspended the use of 2,4,5-T on forests, rights of way and pastures on the basis of a study prompted by complaints from women in Alsea, Ore., that they suffered miscarriages shortly after the herbicide was sprayed near their homes.

Also in 1979 Agent Orange victims formed an organization and launched a class action suit against the manufacturers of the substance. Veterans' groups had been trying for years to get medical care for veterans exposed to Agent Orange in Vietnam, but the Veterans Administration claimed there was not sufficient proof that the chemical was the cause of the veterans' problems. In October 1981, however, Congress passed legislation that among other things authorized medical treatment for veterans suffering from ailments attributed to Agent Orange.

Heavy pesticide use inadvertently created new pest problems for farmers. Some insecticides killed indiscriminately, sometimes disrupting natural controls on potential pest populations. Along with target pests, unselective pesticides may destroy beneficial insects, unleashing new pests that they had preyed on. In response, farmers sometimes have stepped up spraying, applying heavier doses at frequent intervals. "Over the long term, however, this treadmill chemical approach has proved to be self-defeating, only engendering such serious problems as insecticide resistance, human poisonings, and environmental pollution," a 1979 report by the president's Council on Environmental Quality (CEQ) noted.[23]

---

[23] Bottrell, *op. cit.*, p. 13.

Pesticide Controversies

Most ominous of all, some persistent pesticides have spread through the worldwide ecosystem. More than half of a pesticide sprayed from the air drifts off-target and may be carried miles away from the fields. DDT residues have been found in Antarctic penguins and seals, far from the world's farming regions. Long-lasting pesticide residues build up in food chains — for both wildlife and humans. Through a process that biologists call biomagnification, residues accumulate in higher concentrations as they move up through the food chain.

In the past two decades, researchers have documented harmful concentrations of DDT and other chemicals in bald eagles, peregrine falcons, fish and other wildlife. DDT and dieldrin, another long-lasting organochlorine *(see box, p. 48),* slowed reproduction in some threatened bird species by thinning the shells of their eggs. During the 1970s, commercial fishing was suspended in Chesapeake Bay and Lake Ontario after pesticides polluted the waters. The U.S. Department of Agriculture in 1976 paid $3.4 million through a special federal program to compensate honey bee owners whose colonies were poisoned by pesticides. Butterfly collectors contend that specimens have been harder to find since widespread insecticide spraying began.

More than 100,000 Americans a year suffer direct pesticide poisoning, most of them farm workers or workers who handle the chemicals. The accidental death rate has fallen, to 52 people in 1974 from 111 persons in 1961. But the long-term dangers from steady low-level exposure still are being studied.

Alternative Control Methods

FARMERS and chemical industry officials insist that pesticides, properly handled and applied, are both safe and effective. Not all pesticides have been shown to cause harmful side effects, and continued spraying may well be essential if farmers are to continue producing the variety of foods that Americans have grown to like. But doubts about pesticides have sent researchers back to their laboratories and experiment station fields to search for alternative pest management strategies.

Instead of relying on heavy pesticide spraying, some farmers now are experimenting with a combination of pest control methods. Those steps include natural biological controls, cultivation practices, crop rotation, pest-resistant plants, weed-burning, release of sterile insects — along with judicious use of chemical

57

compounds targeted on specific pest species. Since the early 1970s, the Agriculture Department and land grant universities have been encouraging adoption of such integrated pest management (IPM) programs.

Some farmers are reluctant to give up pesticides. But a 1979 study of pest management strategies conducted by the U.S. Office of Technology Assessment found surprisingly wide use of IPM practices, particularly by Great Plains wheat farmers. The report estimated that IPM programs for major U.S. crops could cut pesticide use by up to 75 percent, reduce total pest control costs and still cut pest-caused losses to crops in the field by half.

Some IPM practices amount to what old-timers would call "commonsense farming." Other procedures, involving sophisticated use of natural control agents, have been proven by demonstration projects and successful pest management programs. For instance, release of sterile blowflies has helped suppress screwworm outbreaks in Florida and Southwestern ranching country. Screwworms are blowfly larvae that infest livestock wounds and feed on living tissue. Sterile flies, by mating with fertile populations, reduce the ability of blowflies to reproduce themselves.[24]

Continued Interest in Organic Farming

A few farmers, perhaps 20,000 or so around the nation, avoid using any pesticides at all and follow organic farming methods. Alarmed by environmental pollution, declining soil fertility and rising costs for energy and petroleum-based fertilizers and pesticides, organic farmers rely entirely on natural materials to fertilize the soil and keep pests in check. As a 1980 Agriculture Department study defined them, "to the maximum extent feasible, organic farming systems rely upon crop rotations, crop residues, animal manures, legumes, green manures, off-farm organic wastes, mechanical cultivation, mineral-bearing rocks, and aspects of biological pest control to maintain soil productivity and tilth, to supply plant nutrients, and to control insects, weeds and other pests." [25]

Many experts dismiss organic agriculture as fine for gardens but impractical for large-scale farming operations. The Office of Technology assessment study of pest management strategies for seven major U.S. crops concluded that organic methods offered too little protection against pests. Commercial production of some field crops, including alfalfa and field corn, was possible without synthetic pesticides, the report said, but heavy fruit

---

[24] See R. H. Richardson, J. R. Ellison, W. W. Averhoff, "Autocidal Control of Screwworms in North America," *Science,* Jan. 22, 1982, p. 361.
[25] U.S. Department of Agriculture, "Report on Recommendations on Organic Farming," July 1980, p. xii.

and vegetable losses would make organic production of those crops impossible, while the labor costs of weeding by hand would be prohibitive for most large-scale ventures.

The 1980 Agriculture Department study found a significant number of large farms, even up to 1,500 acres, being farmed organically in the West and Midwest. The survey reported that organic farmers believe they attain yields that match other farms using chemical pesticides in their regions. "Contrary to popular belief," the study added, "most organic farmers have not regressed to agriculture as it was practiced in the 1930s.... Organic farmers still use modern farm machinery, recommended crop varieties, certified seed, sound methods of organic waste management, and recommended soil and water conservation practices."

New Ways of Curbing Predator Losses

In Western ranching states, sheep ranchers have been pressing for years for more effective ways to control coyotes that prey on sheep and lambs. Ever since the Nixon administration ended predator toxicant use on public range lands, sheepmen all over the West have blamed coyotes for livestock losses that have thrown the industry into economic trouble.

President Reagan has reversed Nixon's 1972 executive order, and the Interior Department's Fish and Wildlife Service in November 1981 asked EPA to approve experimental use of Compound 1080 toxicants in collars attached to sheep that were potential coyote victims. The Fish and Wildlife Service, which runs predator trapping programs and other animal damage control efforts, also wants to resume testing of Compound 1080 in small baits that would be less likely to harm other species. Environmentalists have vehemently opposed resumed use of toxicants. But ranchers and predator researchers maintain that the 1972 ban was ordered without sufficient data to prove, one way or the other, whether Compound 1080 was unduly hazardous to eagles and other wildlife.[26]

Since Compound 1080 and other toxicants, including strychnine, were outlawed, ranchers and Fish and Wildlife Service trappers have continued hunting and trapping coyotes. Fish and Wildlife Service marksmen sometimes hunt coyotes from the air if ranchers in an area start suffering serious losses. In 1979, Secretary of the Interior Cecil D. Andrus suspended a practice, known as denning, that burned, gassed or clubbed coyote pups to death in their dens. The Fish and Wildlife Service in 1981 resumed denning on a restricted basis.

[26] See U.S. Fish and Wildlife Service, "Predator Damage in the West: A Study of Coyote Management Alternatives," December 1978.

In the meantime, government and university researchers in Western states have been experimenting with alternative methods, both lethal and non-lethal, for curbing predator losses. Among the measures being studied are training large dogs to guard sheep pastures, installing electrified fences to keep coyotes out, setting off strobe lights and sirens to frighten coyotes off at night, and treating sheep with non-lethal chemicals that produce smells or tastes that repel coyotes. While each of these measures has shown promising results, none has been proven to keep coyotes from killing sheep in all kinds of ranching operations. "There's no one way out there to control livestock losses," Samuel B. Linhart, a biologist at the Fish and Wildlife Service's Denver research center, said in a 1981 interview.

There are no easy answers to the problems of predator and pest control. In order to protect human health and environmental safety, farmers and consumers will continue to pay a price in crop and livestock losses that add billions of dollars to the cost of food.

Selected Bibliography

Books

Brown, A. W. A., *Ecology of Pesticides,* John Wiley & Sons, 1978.
Carson, Rachel, *Silent Spring,* Fawcett Publications, 1962.
Gunn, D. L. and J. G. R. Stevens, *Pesticides and Human Welfare,* Oxford University Press, 1976.
Ordish, George, *The Constant Pest,* Peter Davies, 1976.

Articles

Barnett, Mary and Janet Marinelli, "Medfly Madness," *Environmental Action,* September 1981.
Boraiko, Allen A., "The Pesticide Dilemma," *National Geographic,* February 1980.
Lyman, Francesca, "Industry to Government: 'Let Us Spray,'" *Environmental Action,* November 1981.
Maugh, Thomas H. II, "The Day of the Locusts Is Near," *Science,* Aug. 14, 1981.
Walsh, John, "Medfly Continues to Bug California," *Science,* Dec. 11, 1981.

Reports and Studies

Bottrell, Dale R., "Integrated Pest Management," Council on Environmental Quality, 1979.
U.S. Congress, Office of Technology Assessment, "Pest Management Strategies in Crop Protection," October 1979.
U.S. Department of Agriculture, "Biological Agents in Pest Control," February 1978.

A CID RAIN

by

William Sweet

June 20
1 9 8 0

Editor's Note: U.S.-Canadian negotiations on transboundary air pollution have continued since 1980. Canada's Environment Minister John Roberts announced on Feb. 24, 1982, that his country was "prepared to cut sulfur dioxide emissions in Eastern Canada, including Manitoba, by 50 percent by 1990 contingent on parallel action by the United States." So far, no agreement has been reached. On April 22, 1982, the House Energy and Commerce Committee, which is handling the rewrite of the Clean Air Act *(see p. 68)*, voted to accelerate on-going federal studies of acid rain. But the panel rejected proposals to prevent or limit acid rain.

ACID RAIN

L ITTLE known except among experts just a decade ago, acid rain has emerged as an important and exceptionally challenging environmental problem. Certain substances, primarily sulfur and nitrogen compounds emitted by power plants and smelters, can combine with moisture in the atmosphere or on the surface of the earth to form droplets with a high acid content — sometimes as acidic as vinegar. Though the term "acid rain" has captured the public's imagination, it actually understates the problem. Acid precipitation includes not only rain but also acidified snow, hail and frost, as well as sulfur and nitrogen dust. When sufficiently concentrated, these acids can kill fish and damage material structures. Under certain circumstances they may reduce crop and forest yields and cause or aggravate respiratory diseases in humans.

Since the airborne compounds can travel hundreds and perhaps thousands of miles,[1] ignoring city, state and national boundaries, a solution of the problem will require cooperation among numerous jurisdictions. The temptation to pass the buck will be great, and as concern about acid rain grows, questions will be raised as to whether our political institutions — both national and international — can keep up with unusually rapid advances in knowledge.

In Europe, where acid precipitation has received the most attention, its ill effects have been detected from the Mediterranean basin to the Arctic. Acid is thought to have killed all fishlife in hundreds of lakes in Scandinavia, while in Athens and Rome it has contributed to the disintegration of historic treasures like the Parthenon and Coliseum.[2] In the United States, the acidity of precipitation has increased up to fiftyfold in some parts of the East during the past 25 years, and even in some remote places in the West the rain and snow appear to be getting more acidic at an alarming rate.[3] The greater

---

[1] It has been accepted for some time that pollutants travel from West Germany's industrial heartland to parts of Scandinavia 1,500 kilometers (930 miles) away, and recent evidence suggests that pollutants may blow as far as 10,000 kilometers (6,200 miles). See Richard A. Kerr, "Global Pollution: Is the Arctic Haze Actually Industrial Smog? *Science*, July 20, 1979, pp. 290-293.

[2] See Emily Vermeule, "The Parthenon Is Shrinking," *The Atlantic*, May 1977, pp. 82-85.

[3] See Council on Environmental Quality, *The President's Environmental Program: 1979*, p. 17, and William M. Lewis Jr. and Michael C. Grant, "Acid Precipitation in the Western United States," *Science*, Jan. 11, 1980, pp. 176-177.

acidity is thought to have killed off fish in hundreds of lakes in the northeastern United States and southeastern Canada.

Prevailing westerly winds in the upper atmosphere tend to carry pollutants eastward from the industrialized Great Lakes region *(see maps, p. 75)*. During the summer, especially, pollutants tend to collect over the Great Lakes in high pressure systems — a frequent warm-weather phenomenon in the Midwest. Since winds typically rotate clockwise around high pressure systems, the pollutants gradually are dispersed throughout the Mississippi Valley and along the East Coast.

Appeals for Action by the U.S. and Canada

Last July, scientists told an international commission in Detroit that more than 50,000 lakes in the United States and Canada could become virtually devoid of fish and other aquatic life by 1995.[4] At a meeting held in Toronto in November, some 800 scientists, public officials and environmental activists passed a resolution calling on the United States and Canada "to reduce the overall atmospheric loads of sulfur and nitrogen oxides to less than 50 percent of present levels within 10 years, with regular incremental reductions during that decade."[5] Several governors of Northeastern states who believe their states are suffering from acid rain generated elsewhere have formed a coalition, at the urging of Gov. Hugh L. Carey of New York. They have urged the Environmental Protection Agency to use existing powers more energetically, and they want to amend federal legislation to strengthen controls on acid emissions.

President Carter announced in his 1979 environmental message to Congress a 10-year research program calling for $10 million annual expenditures on acid rain. Canadian environmental officials, concerned that their country receives much more acid precipitation than it sends south, have been pressing the United States to negotiate a strict acid rain treaty. Last July, the two countries issued a statement on trans-boundary air quality which reiterated their commitment, under the Boundary Waters Treaty of 1909, the Great Lakes Water Quality Agreement of 1978 and the Stockholm Declaration on the Human Environment of 1972, to take joint responsibility for solving shared environmental problems.[6]

[4] The U.S.-Canadian International Joint Commission, established to enforce the 1909 Boundary Waters Treaty, monitors water quality throughout the Great Lakes region.
[5] Final Resolution passed by the Action Seminar on Acid Precipitation, Toronto, Nov. 3, 1979. See also Gail Robinson, "Pollution Parley," *Environmental Action,* November 1979, pp. 22-23.
[6] Principle 21 of the 1972 Stockholm Declaration, adopted by delegates of more than 100 countries at the U.N. Conference on the Human Environment, declares: "[S]tates have, in accordance with the Charter of the United Nations and the principles of international law ... the responsibility to ensure that activities within their jurisdiction or control do not cause damage to the environment of other states or areas beyond their limits of national jurisdiction."

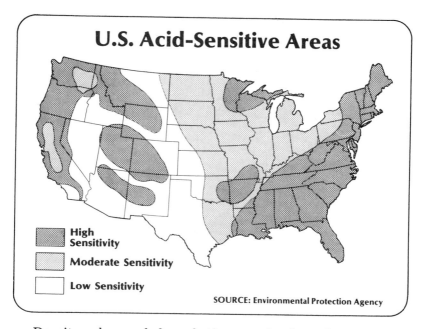

U.S. Acid-Sensitive Areas

High Sensitivity

Moderate Sensitivity

Low Sensitivity

SOURCE: Environmental Protection Agency

Despite solemn pledges, both countries have been accused of dragging their feet, or taking steps that will make the problem worse. U.S. environmentalists claim that Canada's air quality laws are lax and that Ottawa has failed to take strong measures to reduce emissions from the International Nickel Co. smelter at Sudbury, Ontario, which has been called the largest single source of acid pollutants in the world.[7] On the other hand, John Roberts, Canada's environmental minister, has accused the United States of "dumping its garbage over the fence into our country." While he welcomed Carter's research program on acid rain, he said Canadians were "concerned about the lack of speed with which the Carter administration is moving to rectify the problem," and he feared the administration's proposals for increased use of coal would be to "aggravate the acid problem."[8]

Objection to Carter's Coal Conversion Plan

Increased use of coal has been an important objective of U.S. energy policy ever since the government began to formulate a response to rising oil prices. The Energy Supply and Environmental Coordination Act of 1974 authorized the government to order power plants that used oil and gas to burn coal instead. Some 25 Eastern plants soon shifted to coal but half of them soon switched back, largely because clean air standards could be met more easily with oil. In 1978, Congress enacted somewhat tougher coal conversion legislation, which barred new plants

[7] On March 4, the Ontario provincial government offered to order temporary shutdowns of the Inco smelter if this would facilitate negotiations with the United States.
[8] News conference, Washington, D.C., April 18, 1980.

from burning oil and gas, required existing plants to convert by 1990 and authorized the secretary of energy to order individual plants to start burning coal or fuels other than oil and gas.[9]

The Carter administration began ordering plant conversions last fall, but it soon appeared that many utilities could claim exemptions on the ground that they could not afford to make the additional investments required. Because of this, on March 6, the administration proposed new legislation to provide $10 billion in subsidies for coal conversion. In the first phase, the government would provide $3.6 billion to pay half the conversion costs for 107 power plants and $400 million to reduce emissions from plants converting voluntarily. In the second phase, the government would provide $6 billion in grants to encourage voluntary reduction of oil and gas consumption by means of conservation measures or construction of new non-oil burning plants.

On June 11, the Senate Energy Committee approved a coal conversion bill that provides $4.2 billion in subsidies for the first phase of Carter's plan but no authorization for the second phase. The committee rejected an amendment that would have required more stringent emission controls, and some members of Congress believe that coal conversion legislation will not be enacted without stricter environmental restrictions.

Plants burning fossil fuels are the principal source of sulfur emissions in the United States, and environmentalists fear that the Carter "oil backout" plan will aggravate acid pollution. Installations converting to coal apparently would not be subject to EPA's "new source performance standards," which require plants to remove up to 90 percent of the sulfur from coal. Instead, like plants built before 1970, they would be subject to the less stringent ambient air quality standards set out in the Clean Air Act of 1970. Since ambient air quality readings are taken locally and at ground level, utilities and industries are able to meet standards by building tall stacks that disperse pollutants over a wide area. Since the clean air standards went into effect in 1970, over 400 tall stacks have been built in the United States, and of these, 178 are above 500 feet. The tallest stack in the world, 1,200 feet, is at Inco's smelter complex at Sudbury, Ontario.

Tall stacks, in effect, change a local pollution problem into a regional or even international problem. In the Great Lakes region, pollutants tend to collect over the most densely industrialized areas and then gradually disperse until much of the eastern part of the continent is blanketed with acidic clouds.

---

[9] The Powerplant and Industrial Fuel Use Act defined new plants as those on which construction began after April 20, 1977.

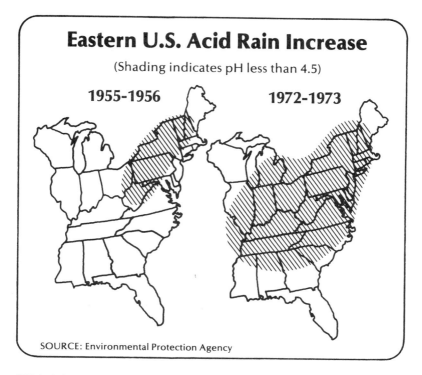

Eastern U.S. Acid Rain Increase

(Shading indicates pH less than 4.5)

1955-1956

1972-1973

SOURCE: Environmental Protection Agency

EPA Administrator Douglas Costle told the Senate subcommittee on the environment on April 21 that coal conversion could send an additional 330,000 tons of sulfur dioxide and 200,000 tons of nitrogen oxide over the Northeast each year.

According to a prestigious study released in May, it will be economic in the coming decades to burn much more coal both in the United States and worldwide while at the same time insisting on strict emission controls. The study said that while acid rain "is acute in some regions and may require early actions by nations in such regions," available technologies can effectively control long-distance airborne pollutants.[10] Representatives of utilities and coal interests argue, on the other hand, that expensive pollution controls should not be required until specific benefits are firmly demonstrated. Jack Kearney of the Edison Electric Institute has said that EPA should be required to show exactly how much effect each added piece of equipment would have on acid precipitation. Senate Majority Leader Robert C. Byrd, D-W.Va., contends that America cannot

---

[10] Cited in *IMF Survey* (publication of the International Monetary Fund), May 19, 1980, p. 154. The World Coal Study was begun in 1978, involved 38 participants from 16 countries and was coordinated by Dr. Carroll L. Wilson of the Massachusetts Institute of Technology. The study said that the only environmental problem that might not be solvable by stricter controls is the possible buildup of carbon dioxide, which may be warming the earth's atmosphere. For background on the so-called "greenhouse" effect, see "America's Coal Economy," *E.R.R.*, 1978 Vol. I, p. 296.

wait to solve the energy problem until the specifics of acid rain are perfectly understood. "EPA has embarked on a 10-year study of acid rain to clarify this area," he said. "Well, we cannot wait 10 years to deal with the energy problem. We know the results of the cost of importing foreign oil in inflation and threats to our national security. We've got to get on with the matter of dealing with imports."[11]

Pressures to Relax Clean Air Standards

By 1990, according to Gus Speth, chairman of the president's Council on Environmental Quality, "plants that are now operating will account for 80 percent of all ... [sulfur dioxide] emissions from coal-fired utilities. And even by 1995 these plants will still account for 73 percent of the ... emissions." Speth reports that emission standards for new automobiles should keep nitrogen emissions from mobile sources at current levels. "[B]ut because the technology for controlling nitrogen oxides from fossil-fuel combustion is not as advanced as sulfur-control technology, the increased use of fossil fuels in power plants over the next two decades will result in a significant increase in nitrogen oxide emissions."[12]

The problem posed by the older plants is especially acute in Ohio, where 21 large coal-burning plants form the most concentrated source of sulfur pollution in this country. In April, a Scientific Advisory Task Force on Acid Rain set up by Ohio Gov. James A. Rhodes recommended that "reasonable, cost-effective efforts be sought to minimize any further increases in 'acid producing' air emissions." As for existing emissions, the study said that "additional research ... is essential prior to formulating public policy which may cause further harm to the present socio-economic conditions of this country."

A report prepared by the Ohio Sierra Club in response to the governor's task force suggested that the state might "take a much more creative role" in attacking the acid rain problem.[13] Such pleas tend to fall on deaf ears. Last year, when Cleveland Electric sought to meet clean air standards at its East Lake and Avon Lake plants by purchasing low-sulfur coal from outside the state, local miners appealed under Section 125 of the 1977 Clean Air Amendments, which authorizes EPA to order a utility to burn locally mined coal if switching fuels would produce unemployment or economic dislocation. Despite objections from the regional EPA office, President Carter announced on June 6, 1979, that standards would be relaxed for the two

[11] Quoted in *The Washington Star,* May 6, 1980.
[12] Gus Speth, "The Sisyphus Syndrome," *National Parks & Conservation Magazine,* February 1980, p. 16.
[13] W. B. Clapham Jr., "Coal, Acid Precipitation and Ohio," a report prepared for the Acid Precipitation Task Force of the Sierra Club, April 23, 1980, summary page.

plants, allowing them to continue burning high-sulfur coal with tall stacks and without scrubbers.

In an unexpected about-face, the EPA on June 17 announced tighter standards for the plants, including for the first time the possibility of imposing limits on the height of smokestacks. Robert W. Flacke, commissioner of New York's Environmental Conservation Department, accuses EPA of "inconsistency" — of enforcing a strict tall-stacks policy in one region but not another.[14] EPA's defenders say that the agency will not be able to move effectively against acid rain until clean air legislation is tightened. Frances Dubrowski of the Natural Resources Defense Council agrees that better legislation is required but also argues that EPA could do much more under existing authority to curb acid emissions.

Some environmentalists fear that Congress will weaken the Clean Air Act when it comes up for reauthorization next year, especially since Edmund G. Muskie has left the Senate and his chairmanship of the Subcommittee on Environmental Pollution to become secretary of state. But Dubrowski thinks the Clean Air Act is more likely to be strengthened than weakened,[15] and Speth hopes Muskie will bring a stronger environmental perspective to U.S. foreign policy. "I am very excited about Muskie's coming on board because we and the State Department will be working closely in the coming months on a significant list of global environmental problems," Speth said.[16]

Dispute Over Extent of Scientific Evidence

Ralph M. Perhac of the Electric Power Research Institute testified March 19 before the Senate subcommittee that the scientific evidence on acid rain is incomplete and ambiguous. According to Perhac, the data on acid rain which scientists began to collect in the early 1950s show no consistent trend. While there was a sharp increase in measured acidity in the mid-1960s, Perhac said, the change is unexplained and might have resulted from modified measurement techniques. Arguing that humidity, temperature and wind patterns may have more influence on acid precipitation than emissions do, Perhac counseled against imposing expensive controls until their precise benefits could be assessed.

"I cannot overemphasize the importance of knowing what responsibility the industry has for acid deposition," Perhac told the subcommittee. "Unless we know that, we cannot judge the efficacy of any control strategy which might be promulgated and, as scientists, we have an obligation to evaluate the extent to which a control strategy will achieve its goal. For acid precipi-

[14] Interview, May 28, 1980.
[15] Interview, May 13, 1980.
[16] Quoted in *The New York Times,* May 9, 1980.

tation, we cannot do that. For example, we cannot tell you if a certain reduction, say 20 percent, in . . . [sulfur dioxide] emissions will reduce the acidity of rain."

G. W. Barrett of England's Central Electricity Generating Board made similar points in testimony to the Allegheny County (Pa.) State Implementation Plan Hearing on March 25 in Pittsburgh. Like Perhac, he stressed the inadequacy of the monitoring systems, pointed out that there are very wide unexplained variations in annual acidity records — sometimes as much as four to one — and described natural events that might account for effects attributed to acid rain. Some scientists suspect that the rise in acidity measured in the 1960s was as large as it seemed only because the atmosphere was exceptionally alkaline during the 1950s, when drought conditions produced an unusual amount of air-borne calcium.

Kenneth Hood, an acid rain expert with the Council on Environmental Quality, has said: "The evidence may not be as extensive as we would like, and it may turn out that Mr. Perhac is accurate. But if we wait until damage is so evident that everybody can perceive it, then we may already be beyond the point of no return." Hood said it is "better to discover that the patient is not as sick as you thought than to wait, doing nothing, and then see him die."[17]

Advancing Research on Acid Rain

A BRITISH study published in 1911 connected acidic precipitation with coal combustion in the industrial city of Leeds.[18] The discovery attracted little attention at the time, however, and it was not until well after World War II that scientists began a systematic study of the chemistry and effects of acid rain. By the early 1960s, a confluence of seemingly unrelated research in agriculture, atmospheric science and limnology — the study of lakes — established acid precipitation as a serious environmental problem.

Probably the most important data on acid precipitation developed from the work of a Swedish soil scientist, Hans Egner, at an agricultural college near Uppsala. Hoping to gather data on the fertilization of crops by atmospheric nutrients, Egner

---

[17] Interview, May 2, 1980.
[18] The authors, C. Crowther and H. G. Ruston, mistakenly attributed the acid to sulfur, rather than to the high chlorine content of English coal, according to Ellis B. Cowling, *From Research to Public Policy: Progress in Scientific and Public Understanding of Acid Precipitation and Its Biological Effects* (1980), p. 11.

set up a network to sample precipitation all over Sweden. This network, which soon spread to Norway, Denmark, Finland and finally most of Europe, eventually was to provide the first information on changes in the acidity of precipitation. The International Meteorological Institute in Stockholm took over management of the network in 1956.

Using the data from Egner's network, two other Swedish scientists, Karl Gustav Rossby and Erik Ericksson, showed that atmospheric pollutants could travel hundreds of miles from their source. Their studies, together with a series of papers published in the late 1950s and early 1960s by Eville Gorham, provided the basis for understanding how acid rain is generated and dispersed. Working in England and Canada, Gorham and his colleagues found that abnormally acidic precipitation could be attributed to combustion of fossil fuels and that changes in lake and soil chemistry could be traced to the precipitation.

According to a leading U.S. authority on acid rain, Ellis B. Cowling of North Carolina State University, Gorham had established by the early 1960s "a major part of our understanding of the sources . . . and ecological significance of acidity in precipitation. But these pioneering researches were met by a thundering silence from both the scientific community and the public at large. . . . Whatever the reason, this lack of recognition resulted in at least a 10-year lag in both scientific and public awareness of acid precipitation and its ecological significance."[19]

Wider Understanding of Acid Precipitation

Wider appreciation of the acid problem came only when Svante Odén, a young colleague of Egner, Rossby and Ericksson, published a comprehensive story on acid precipitation in *Dagens Nyheter,* a leading Swedish newspaper, in 1967. According to Cowling, Odén's "analysis of air-mass trajectories clearly showed that acid precipitation was a large-scale regional phenomenon in much of Europe, that both precipitation and surface waters were becoming more acidic, and that long-distance . . . transport of both sulfur- and nitrogen-containing air pollutants was occurring among the various nations of Europe." Because of southern Scandinavia's special vulnerability to acid rain from England and Western Europe, Odén's article attracted wide attention, and the Swedish government initiated an inquiry which led eventually to a presentation at the United Nations Conference on the Human Environment in 1972.[20]

---

[19] *Ibid.,* p. 12.
[20] See B. Bolin, et al., *Sweden's Case Study for the United Nations Conference on the Human Environment: Air Pollution Across National Boundaries* (1971).

Excess acidity in precipitation, as scientists have come to understand the problem, arises primarily from the reaction of sulfur and nitrogen oxides with water.[21] This process of oxidation can take place either in the atmosphere or after sulfates and nitrates are deposited in the lakes or the soil. Numerous factors such as the intensity of sunlight can influence the type of reaction that takes place and the speed with which sulfuric and nitric acids are formed. Since atmospheric conditions also have a strong effect on the concentration and dispersal of pollutants, severe cases of acid deposition tend to occur in fits and starts and for this reason may be amenable to episodic control — temporary shutdowns of plants, for example.

The acidity of precipitation and of waters or soil contaminated by pollutants is measured on the pH scale, which ranges from 0 to 14. The lower values signify acidity and the higher values alkalinity, while a reading of 7 is neutral. Since the scale is logarithmic, a change in one point on the scale indicates a tenfold change in acidity. Thus, if the acidity of rainfall drops from 5.6, its average natural level, to 4.6, then it has become 10 times more acidic. A drop to 3.6 would signify it had become 100 times more acidic.

The sensitivity of freshwater systems to acid precipitation depends largely on their buffering capacity, that is, their ability to neutralize acids. When the bedrock under lakes or streams consists largely of siliceous types such as granite and quartz, the water generally is highly sensitive to added acid. The measured pH of a lake may remain relatively constant as acid precipitation rises, as long as bicarbonate is available, but once the lake's buffering capacity is exhausted a sudden and sharp drop in pH may be registered.[22]

Siliceous bedrock is found in Scandinavia, New England, the Adirondacks and the Appalachians, precisely the areas where drastic changes in lake ecology have been detected.[23] Adding to the vulnerability of mountainous and northern regions is the so-called "acid shock" phenomenon. Acid collects with the snows of winter and reaches the streams and lakes during the spring runoff just when fish are spawning, an exceptionally sensitive stage in the aquatic life cycle.

Richard J. Beamish, a scientist who has studied lakes around Canada's Sudbury smelter complex, found that adult fish become emaciated and deformed as acidity rises. Eggs may de-

---

[21] There are other artificial or "anthropogenic" sources of acid rain, however. Some coal-fired plants, for example, emit hydrochloric acid directly.
[22] See Norman R. Glass, et al., "Effects of Acid Precipitation," *Environmental Science & Technology*, November 1979, p. 1353.
[23] See Gene E. Likens, et al., "Acid Rain," *Scientific American*, October 1979, pp. 43-51.

Natural Causes of Acid Rain

The main contibutor to the natural acidity of precipitation, which averages about 5.6 on the pH scale, is carbon dioxide. Just as sulfur and nitrogen oxides combine with moisture to form sulfuric and nitric acids, carbon dioxide generates carbonic acid in the presence of water. Many other substances entering the atmosphere may affect precipitation pH. Unusually large amounts of dust and soil debris, for example, tend to make precipitation more alkaline than average.

Since volcanic eruptions constitute a significant natural source of sulfur oxides and acids, experts on precipitation chemistry are beginning to turn their attention to the activity at Mount St. Helens. People in the vicinity of the volcano reported smelling sulfur before the big eruptions on May 18. Residents of some towns where ash has fallen also say they detected the telltale odor of rotten eggs. The initial measurements indicate, nonetheless, that acid emissions from Mount St. Helens are relatively small. In some areas around the volcano, wildflowers already are sprouting through the ash — a good sign of low acidity, according to chemists and biologists.

velop but never pass from the ovary to be fertilized. As the pH drops, small-mouth bass and walleyes are eliminated first, then northern pike and lake trout start to die, and finally even the acid-resistant herring, perch and rock bass succumb.[24] Ann Henriksen, a scientist at the Norwegian Institute for Water has estimated that fish will be eliminated when the long-term average pH of precipitation drops below 4.3.

Tracking Air Pollutants for Long Distances

In 1968 the Swedish scientist Odén reported that an area of high acidity — 4 to 4.5 on the pH scale as measured by the European Air Chemistry Network — had spread from Belgium, the Netherlands and Luxembourg in the late 1950s to most of Germany, northern France, the eastern British Isles and southern Scandinavia by the late 1960s. Mounting concern about acid rain prompted the multinational Organization for Economic Cooperation and Development to launch a program in 1972 to measure the long-range movement of air pollutants. As reported in 1977, the program "confirmed that sulfur compounds do travel long distances (several hundred kilometers or more) in the atmosphere" and showed that "the air quality in any one European country is measurably affected by emissions from other European countries."

The study reported that sulfur deposits were usually heaviest in industrial areas where emissions were great. But localized areas of southern Scandinavia and Switzerland subject to heavy snowfall suffered more damage than some heavily industrialized

[24] See James Gannon, "Acid Rain Fallout: Pollution & Politics," *The Environmental Journal,* October 1978, pp. 15-21.

areas far away. The study showed that in half the countries, the major part of total estimated depositions in 1974 originated from foreign emissions.[25]

This kind of long-distance tracking in North America has lagged well behind European efforts. Before 1954 no measurement of precipitation pH is known to have been published in the United States, and the first regional monitoring of precipitation chemistry took place between 1953 and 1955. The U.S. Public Health Service and the National Center for Atmospheric Research established the first nationwide monitoring system in 1959. About the same time scientists initiated studies at Hubbard Brook Experimental Farm in New Hampshire.[26]

The Canadian Network for Sampling Precipitation began operating in 1976, and in 1978 the U.S. government initiated the National Atmospheric Deposition Program — a much more comprehensive monitoring system than had existed previously. Acting on the recommendation of a study commissioned by the Council on Environmental Quality, President Carter announced in his environmental message of Aug. 2, 1979, the establishment of a Federal Acid Rain Coordination Committee. Directed jointly by EPA and the Department of Agriculture, the committee is to manage the federal research program.

International Sharing of Research Findings

During the past year there have been numerous acid rain conferences, some to provide officials and environmentalists with an opportunity to coordinate strategy and issue calls for action, others to give scientists a chance to exchange new research results. One of the most heavily attended meetings took place in March in Sandefjord, Norway, under the sponsorship of Norway's "SNSF Project" — a government program known by its Norwegian initials. It was started in 1972 to study the effects of acid rain on forests, fish, soil, vegetation and water.

Among the results described at such conferences and in the scientific literature, perhaps the most important concerns the leaching of metals in soil and water. Research has shown that acid pollutants can react with otherwise-inert metals and mobilize them into an ecosystem. Joan P. Baker and Carl L. Schofield reported at Sandefjord, for example, that elevated levels of aluminum in surface waters "appear to have serious effects on fish at pH levels above those which are normally considered harmful for most aquatic biota."[27] If toxic metals

[25] Organization for Economic Cooperation and Development, *The OECD Programme on Long-Range Transport of Air Pollutants: Summary Report* (1979), pp. 9-10.
[26] See Danny L. Rambo, *Interim Report: Acid Precipitation in the United States* (1978), pp. 2-3, and Cowling, *op. cit.*, pp. 16-17.
[27] Joan P. Baker and Carl L. Schofield, "Aluminum Toxicity to Fish as Related to Acid Precipitation and Adirondack Surface Water Quality," *Abstracts of Voluntary Contributions: Sandefjord Conference*, v. 1 (1980).

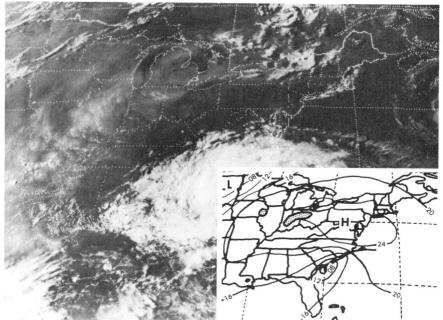

Pollutants trapped in a stagnant high pressure system form an aerosol haze, concentrated on Aug. 20, 1976, south of the Great Lakes

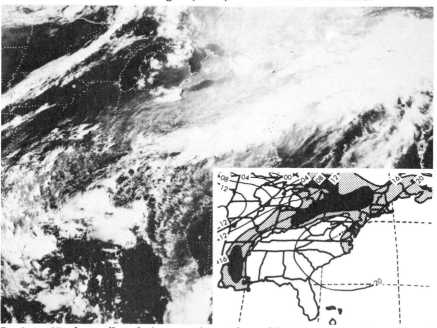

By Aug. 27, the polluted air extends northward into Canada and southward into the lower Mississippi River valley

such as mercury are leached into a water system and absorbed by fish, then the metals may concentrate in the food chain and eventually pose a serious hazard to human health. The Ministry of the Environment in Ontario has issued a "Guide to Eating Ontario Sport Fish" which states that some 70 percent of the province's lakes have at least some contaminated fish that are unsafe to eat.

Because of the complexity of terrestrial ecosystems, the effects of acid rain on crop and forest yields are just beginning to be understood. But studies indicate that acid rain can lower crop yields by eliminating micro-organisms that retain nitrogen necessary for plant growth, by leaching out plant nutrients, and by disfiguring crops. One expert has summarized the effects in the following terms: "[A]cid rain leaches nutrients such as calcium and potassium from the plant tissues, causes lesions and deformities in the foliage, and erodes the waxy coating which helps protect the foliage against disease and water stress. . . . Metals such as aluminum, manganese, iron, mercury, cadmium, and lead are mobilized in toxic quantities and made available for root absorption. Thus, the foliage is assaulted from above while the roots are starved and poisoned from below."[28]

The direct effects of acid precipitation on human health are poorly understood, but an association with acid pollutants — notably dry sulfur depositions — appears to be firmly established.[29] Toxic metals leached by acid rain may also accumulate in the food chain and lead to disorders of the nervous system, kidney, liver, and heart.[30]

Solving the Acid Rain Problem

RESEARCH programs on acid rain are well established at several universities, notably Cornell, North Carolina State, Minnesota and Virginia; at EPA laboratories at Corvallis, Ore., Duluth, Minn., and Research Triangle Park, N.C.; and at a multitude of other institutions such as the Illinois State Water Survey. During the coming decade these programs should help

---

[28] Norman R. Glass, "Mounting Acid Rain," *EPA Journal*, July-August 1979, p. 27. Dr. Glass is director of the Terrestrial Systems Division of EPA's Experimental Research Laboratory at Corvallis, Ore.

[29] See L. D. Hamilton, "Health Effects of Acid Precipitation," report on research done by Brookhaven National Laboratory for the Department of Energy, presented at the Action Seminar on Acid Precipitation, Toronto, Ontario, Nov. 1-3, 1979, pp. 4 and 6.

[30] See Shepherd Ogden, "Fact Sheet: What Is Acid Rain," Congressional Environmental Study Conference, April 30, 1980.

resolve many of the ecological and economic issues raised by acid rain. In the meantime, however, there will be a need to take remedial and preventive actions where detrimental effects already are firmly demonstrated.

Scandinavia, Switzerland and eastern North America have proved to be highly vulnerable to acid precipitation for a number of reasons: their location in the paths typically taken by winds carrying pollutants; their high precipitation rates; the low buffering capacity of their soils and waters; and their vulnerability to the acid-shock phenomenon. Because of the possibility that acidity levels may mount very sharply once buffering capacity is exhausted, these regions could suffer abrupt and irreversible damage if prompt action is not taken.

As a stopgap measure, various authorities including New York state have dumped lime into lakes in order to bolster their buffering capacity. But according to New York's environmental commissioner, Robert W. Flacke, liming is "not very effective and quite costly." He said the state has had to concentrate available funds on saving unique native trout. Many scientists, environmentalists and public officials believe that it is urgently necessary to attack the causes as well as the symptoms of acid rain.

Anti-Pollution Technology for Coal Burning

One approach to reducing levels of acid rain is to make coal combustion cleaner — by preparing coal before burning, by making the combustion process more efficient, or by cleansing the emissions after combustion. Technologies for removing sulfur are relatively advanced and can reduce the amount emitted by a plant by as much as 90 percent. Flue gas desulfurization, or "scrubbing," is the technology most widely used but preparation of coal before combustion is receiving increased attention. Coal cleaning can remove up to 40 percent of the sulfur from high-sulfur coal, leading to reduced scrubbing costs and greater economic viability for regions that produce high-sulfur coal.[31] According to an article published by the Electric Power Research Institute, "A tangle of developing circumstances — including higher coal prices, diminishing coal quality, increasing coal use, and mounting environmental awareness — are tipping the balance in favor of coal cleaning in many cases."[32]

The technology for elimination of nitrogen emissions from stationary sources such as power plants is less advanced than

---

[31] See paper prepared by James D. Kilgroe, "Coal Cleaning for Sulfur Oxide Emission Control," presented at the Acid Rain Conference, Springfield, Va., April 8-9, 1980.
[32] Kurt E. Yeager, "More Coal Per Ton," *EPRI Journal*, June 1979, p. 7.

for sulfur emissions and currently can achieve reductions of about 30 percent. Thus nitrogen oxide emissions from stationary sources may rise substantially in the years ahead. Since coal-cleaning is expensive, a case can be made for a much more concerted effort at energy conservation. The demand for energy during the Seventies grew at less than half the Fifties' and Sixties' rate, and growth could be even slower in this decade and the next if energy prices continue to rise or even stay at present levels. If so, emissions of acid pollutants may increase at a much slower pace than is sometimes predicted.

If, on the other hand, energy demand begins to grow once again, nuclear energy may become a more popular alternative to coal. In Sweden, the publicity given the acid rain problem figured prominently in the debate that led up to a national referendum on nuclear energy on March 23. Despite the stir that the Three Mile Island accident had caused in Sweden, voters delivered a stronger endorsement of nuclear power than had been generally expected.[33]

Cleanup Barriers: Cost, Energy and Politics

Regardless of how new emissions of acid pollutants are prevented or reduced, there will remain the problem posed by existing plants. Annual emissions of sulfur in the United States are estimated at about 30 million tons, and nitrogen emissions at 20 million tons.[34] Sulfur levels are expected to stay roughly constant or to drop as older power plants are decommissioned, while nitrogen emissions increase about 50 percent.

Efforts to rid existing facilities of pollutants run up against the opposition of those who would have to pay the bill. In Midwestern states such as Ohio and Illinois, which are highly dependent on locally mined high sulfur coal, there naturally is resistance to tight standards entailing high costs. But special exemptions for such states invariably draw protests from areas that are forced to comply without exemption. New York's environmental authorities insist that a single national standard for coal emissions is the only fair procedure, and Flacke advocates — as an alternative to Carter's coal-conversion subsidies to utilities — federal support for pre-combustion preparation of high-sulfur coal.

The establishment of an international policy on acid rain involves even more complications. Last November, 35 nations, including the United States, signed an international convention on trans-boundary pollution. It called for joint research and

---

[33] See *Current Sweden,* published by the Swedish Institute, May 1979 (No. 223) and February 1980 (Nos. 245 and 246).
[34] See the Office of Technology Assessment, *The Direct Use of Coal* (1979), pp. 188-189, and Environmental Protection Agency, *Research Summary: Acid Rain* (1979), p. 1.

Coal Cleaning Technologies: Effectiveness and Costs

	Percent of Pollutant Removed	Capital Cost $/KW	Annual Operating Cost Mills/KWH
Sulfur Control			
Low-Sulfur Coal			
Conventional Scrubbing	70	120	7.0
Dry Scrubbing	70	85	4.7
High-Sulfur Coal			
Physical Coal Cleaning	40	34	2.7
Conventional Scrubbing	90	175	9.1
Nitrogen Control			
Existing Technologies			
Modern Burner Design	30	4.2	0.11
Staged Combustion	30	3.0	0.10
Anticipated New Technologies			
For Wall-Fired Burners	70-80	—	—
For Tangentially Fired Burners	60-75	—	—

Source: Steve R. Reznek, "Emissions Control: Technology and Costs," and fact sheet on nitrogen exoides, U.S. EPA presentations at Springfield, Va., conference, April 8, 1980.

monitoring, but did not set firm goals, limits or timetables for controlling sulfur pollutants. One U.S. participant described it as "having jaws and perhaps the beginning of a tooth."[35]

Writing in the July-August issue of *Science 80,* Armin Rosencranz of the Environmental Law Institute characterized the prospects for effective international action on acid rain as "bleak." He said that West Germany has resisted strengthening their environmental laws to placate their neighbors, while the British have been "publicly skeptical about the urgency and the supposed irreversibility of the acid rain problem." As for North America, "Canadian-U.S. negotiators are far from a formal agreement after 18 months of talks."

---

[35] Quoted by Dianne Dumanoski, *Boston Globe,* Nov. 19, 1980.

Selected Bibliography

Articles

"Acid from the Sky," *Mosaic,* July-August 1979, pp. 35-40.

Brezonik, Patrick L., et al., "Acid Precipitation and Sulfate Deposition in Florida," *Science,* May 30, 1980, pp. 1027-1029.

Dumanoski, Dianne, series on acid rain in the *Boston Globe,* Nov. 18-19, Dec. 30-31, 1979.

Gannon, James, "Acid Rain Fallout: Pollution and Politics," *The Environmental Journal,* October 1978.

Glass, Norman R., "Mounting Acid Rain," *EPA Journal,* July-August 1979, pp. 25-27.

——et al., "Effects of Acid Precipitation," *Environmental Science & Technology,* November 1979.

Kerr, Richard A., "Global Pollution: Is the Arctic Haze Actually Industrial Smog?" *Science,* July 20, 1979, pp. 290-293.

Likens, Gene E. et al., "Acid Rain," *Scientific American,* October 1979.

Speth, Gus, "The Sisyphus Syndrome: Acid Rain and Public Responsibility," *National Parks & Conservation Magazine,* February 1980, pp. 12-17.

Yeager, Kurt E., "More Coal Per Ton," *EPRI* [Electric Power Research Institute] *Journal,* June 1979, pp. 2-13.

Reports and Studies

Altshuller, A. P. and McBean, G. A., "The LRTAP Problem in North America: A Preliminary Overview," prepared by the United States-Canada Research Consultation Group on the Long-Range Transport of Air Pollutants.

Clapham, W. B. Jr., "Coal, Acid Precipitation, and Ohio," prepared for the Acid Precipitation Task Force of the Sierra Club, Cleveland, Ohio, April 23, 1980.

Cowling, Ellis B., "From Research to Public Policy: Progress in Scientific and Public Understanding of Acid Precipitation and Its Biological Effects," School of Forest Resources, North Carolina State University, 1980.

Environmental Protection Agency, "Research Summary: Acid Rain," EPA-600/8-79-028, Washington, D. C., October 1979.

——"Research Summary: Controlling Nitrogen Oxides," EPA-600/8-80-004, February 1980.

Federal Interagency Committee on the Health and Environmental Effects of Energy Technologies, "Health and Environmental Effects of Coal Technologies," DOE/HEW/EPA-04, Washington, D.C., August 1979.

Hamilton, L. D., "Health Effects of Acid Precipitation," report on Brookhaven National Laboratory research, presented at the Action Seminar on Acid Precipitation, Toronto, Canada, Nov. 1-3, 1979.

Kilgroe, James D., "Coal Cleaning for Sulfur Oxide Emission Control," paper presented at EPA's Acid Rain Conference, Springfield, Va., April 8-9, 1980.

Ogden, Shepherd, "Fact Sheet: What Is Acid Rain," Environmental Study Conference, U.S. Congress, April 30, 1980.

Organization for Economic Cooperation and Development, "The OECD Programme on Long-Range Transport of Air Pollutants: Summary Report," Paris, France, 1979.

Noise control

by

Marc Leepson

Feb. 22
1 9 8 0

Editor's Note: During his 1980 presidential campaign Ronald Reagan repeatedly promised to abolish regulations that were hampering U.S. businesses, or to turn enforcement over to the states. One of his first such efforts was a March 10, 1981, budget proposal to phase out the Environmental Protection Agency's noise control program by 1982. Reagan proposed to leave federal regulations issued under the Noise Control Act of 1972 on the books, but to provide no money for federal enforcement. This provoked a flurry of opposition from manufacturers of railroad and trucking equipment who argued that without federal noise regulations they would be subject to standards that could vary from state to state and city to city.

Both houses of Congress decided to continue some form of federal noise control program, but differences between House and Senate bills were not ironed out when this book went to press in late April 1982. EPA's noise control program is operating under a continuing resolution that provides some $2 million for fiscal year 1982, about $11 million less than the Carter administration's 1981 appropriation.

The Reagan administration's proposed budget for fiscal year 1983 contained no funds for noise control. The Occupational Safety and Health Administration's workplace noise standard of 90 decibels for eight hours remains in place, although the agency still is considering lowering the standard to 85 decibels *(see pp. 86-87).*

NOISE CONTROL

THE U.S. DEPARTMENT of Housing and Urban Development conducts a survey every year to find out what city residents dislike about their living environment.[1] Each year since 1973 the same condition has been named most undesirable. It is not crime, air pollution or traffic congestion. It is noise — an undesirable ingredient not only of city life but also of life in the suburbs and even rural areas. A trip to the suburbs may leave behind the city's jackhammers, pile drivers and traffic noises, but other assaults on the ear lie waiting outside city limits. "The kid next door is engaged in an exotic activity called motorcycle 'scrambling,' the neighbor across the street is shaving half an inch off his golf course greens with a power lawn mower," wrote Deborah Baldwin, an editor of *Environmental Action* magazine, "the washing machine is rattling into the spin cycle, and an 80-pound German shepherd out back is trying to get a bark in sideways lest anyone forget his supper."[2]

Noise is everywhere today, but noise control is but a minor element of the nation's anti-pollution efforts at the federal, state and local levels. The U.S. Environmental Protection Agency (EPA) is currently spending $14 million a year — about 1 percent of its total budget — to try to reduce noise. It can be argued that noise control should be only a small part of the government's anti-pollution programs. After all, noise is a relatively mild form of pollution when compared to the well-known dangers of air and water pollution. Moreover, citizens' outcries against excessive noise tend to be localized and rarely develop political clout.

Nonetheless, noise problems have commanded enough attention in recent years to impel Congress to act. It has provided money and technical assistance to communities for noise control programs, and federal agencies established by Congress have sought to regulate noise levels in the workplace and to set noise standards for aircraft, trucks, motorcycles, some construction equipment and even power lawn mowers. Since noise regulation usually means added expenses for the affected industries, they frequently come to Congress seeking relief. To cite a recent example, Congress on Feb. 5 cleared a compromise bill to delay some of the noise-control rules for commercial airlines *(see p.*

---

[1] The latest survey, for 1978, is titled "Undesirable Neighborhood Conditions, United States."

[2] Deborah Baldwin, "No Noise is Good Noise," *Environmental Action*, July 1, 1978, p. 4.

94). Despite the difficulty in mandating noise control, the thrust for doing so lies in the growing public awareness that excessive noise may be harmful to health.

Deafness From Urban Din, Rock Music

It has been long recognized that prolonged exposure to noises such as highly amplified music or the roar of jet engines can result in permanent damage to hearing. But it has come to light recently that noise is suspected of leading to a host of physiological and psychological problems from irritability to heart disease. The most obvious danger to health posed by noise is hearing loss. The EPA estimates that some 20 million Americans are subjected to noise levels that could permanently damage their hearing, and about 18 million have some hearing loss due to noise exposure.

Hearing loss takes place in the seat of the inner ear in the thousands of small, extremely sensitive hair-like cells of the cochlea. These cells vibrate when exposed to sound, sending impulses to higher nerve centers where the impulses are perceived as sound. When loud sounds damage the cochlea's cells, the harm is irreparable. Hearing loss usually is a gradual process, and very often the victim does not notice the initial stages of deafness. Relatively continuous exposure to sound exceeding 70 decibels *(see opposite page)* can result in hearing loss. Such sound levels are often emitted by ordinary highway traffic, a noisy restaurant or a television set.

Medical researchers are studying what happens to hearing when a person is exposed to sound levels much higher than 70 decibels for long periods of time. One area of research has concentrated on rock musicians and their listeners. Music from the loudest rock bands averages about 110 decibels, and can reach 130 decibels is discos. Audiologists began studying the effects of loud rock music on both performers and listeners a decade ago. Tests at that time indicated that both groups suffered measurable hearing losses after exposure to loud rock concerts.

More recent tests on listeners and performers have come up with different conclusions. The first long-term study of noise-induced hearing among rock musicians was begun in 1967 by William F. Rintelmann, professor and chairman of audiology at the University of Pennsylvania School of Medicine. He told *Rolling Stone* magazine recently: "We found over a seven-year period that four of the six musicians' [exposed to about 105 decibels for an average of 11 hours a week for three years] hearing had not changed. One musician showed a very mild high-frequency loss, but it was still within normal limits. The other had a slight hearing loss. That leads us to say that there's a certain amount

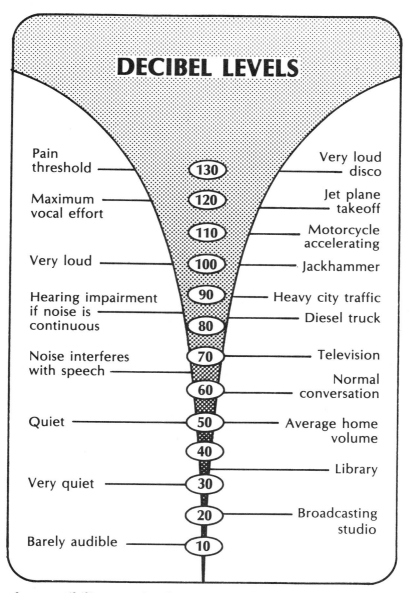

DECIBEL LEVELS

Pain threshold	130	Very loud disco
Maximum vocal effort	120	Jet plane takeoff
	110	Motorcycle accelerating
Very loud	100	Jackhammer
Hearing impairment if noise is continuous	90	Heavy city traffic
	80	Diesel truck
Noise interferes with speech	70	Television
	60	Normal conversation
Quiet	50	Average home volume
	40	
		Library
Very quiet	30	
	20	Broadcasting studio
Barely audible	10	

of susceptibility to noise damage from rock music, but it's not dramatic."[3]

The Noise Factor in Stress and Anxiety

"Noise has been clearly identified as an important cause of physical and psychological stress," the EPA has said, "and stress has been directly linked with many of our most common health problems."[4] Stress can lead to high blood pressure,

[3] Rintelmann was quoted in the magazine's Feb. 7, 1980, issue.
[4] Environmental Protection Agency, "Noise: A Health Problem," August 1978, p. 23.

insomnia, migraine headaches, ulcers, digestive disorders, alcoholism, anxiety, and a host of other ills.

Noise-related stress can aggravate existing emotional disorders. Several studies have found that prolonged exposure to noise can lead to a greater incidence of psychological problems in factory workers.[5] Excessive noise also can lead to increases in adrenaline flow, elevated heart rates and blood pressure — three factors that are associated with heart disease. Excessive noise can also cause special problems with children. It can impair language development and reading ability. Researchers are especially concerned with the effect of noise on the unborn.

Fetuses are not fully protected from their mothers' responses to stress — whether that stress is caused by loud noises or other factors. Studies of pregnant women in the United States, Britain and Japan have indicated that there is a higher incidence of birth defects among women living near airport runways. A study conducted by F. Nowell Jones, a psychology professor at UCLA (University of California at Los Angeles), and Judy Tauscher of the UCLA School of Public Health, found the rate of abnormal births to be significantly higher among women living in an area under the landing pattern of Los Angeles International Airport than in the rest of Los Angeles County.

As the various studies indicate, noise is not solely an American problem. According to a 1979 United Nations report, noise from automobiles, motorcycles and trucks creates a problem throughout the world, especially in the highly industrial sections of Europe and Japan. Mostafa Tolba, executive director of the U.N. Environment Programme, wrote last year: "Surveys carried out in the United Kingdom, France, Japan and Sweden show not only that traffic is considered to generate the most annoying kind of noise, but that it is often one of the most serious problems that town-dwellers must face."[6] According to U.N. figures, the number of motor vehicles in the world at the close of the 1970s exceeded 300 million, up from 100 million in 1960 and 200 million in 1970.

Setting Decibel Levels for the Workplace

Those who work in the construction, lumber, mining, steel and textile industries are especially exposed to loud noises. The federal agency that oversees safety and health on the job — the Occupational Safety and Health Administration (OSHA) — currently sets the standard of noise for any workplace at 90 decibels. This means that if the noise level exceeds 90 decibels for eight hours a day or rises even higher for a shorter time, the

[5] The studies are cited in "Noise: A Health Problem."

[6] Tolba's report was published, in part, in *UN Chronicle*, July 1979. The report, issued June 5, 1979, by the U.N. Environment Programme, is titled "State of the World Environment."

Government-Mandated Permissible Noise Levels in the Workplace		
Hours Per Day	**Decibel Sound Level**	
8	90	
6	92	
4	95	
3	97	
2	100	
1-1/2	102	
1	105	
1/2	110	
1/4 or less	115	

workers are "overexposed." At that point, the agency calls for "feasible" engineering or administrative controls to reduce the noise level.

"By 'feasible' engineering controls we mean design changes," explained Richard J. Peppin, senior scientist at OSHA's Health Standards Office. "This could mean changing the gears of a machine or putting enclosures around it. Administrative controls essentially mean to rotate employees so that if they're exposed to say 95 decibels for eight hours, you get them so that they are there for only four hours. . . . Sometimes that works out but sometimes people are skilled at a certain job and they can't do that."[7] If the company cannot make the needed engineering or administrative changes, OSHA recommends that they outfit the exposed workers with such protective devices as earcuffs (the headphone-like devices worn by airport workers) or earplugs.

Since 1974, OSHA has considered a proposal to lower the permissible eight-hour noise level from 90 to 85 decibels. The proposal, predictably, draws the support of labor groups and the opposition of business groups. Much of the opposition centers on a 1976 study by the agency which estimated that businesses would have to pay about $18.5 billion in engineering controls to reach the 85 decibel level.

Although OSHA officials say the new standard could be put into effect by the end of the year, labor leaders do not disguise their irritation over the long delay. "They have to do something - or someone's going to take them to court," Eric Frumin of the Amalgamated Clothing and Textile Workers Union said last year. "When something has hung around as long as this particular issue, even a decision that you are not going to do anything or very little is better than no apparent decision."[8]

[7] Interview, Jan. 29, 1980.
[8] Quoted in *Business Week*, March 26, 1979, p. 30.

Regulations to Control Noise

COMPLAINTS about excessive noise seem to be as old as city living. Julius Caesar figured in a controversy over urban noise 20 centuries ago. After barring chariots from the streets of Rome by day as a safety measure, he was forced to exclude them by night because the first edict resulted in a great increase of sleep-disturbing clatter in the city's streets. Street noises in London of the 1890s have been described as raising a "din that . . . is beyond conception. It was not any such paltry thing as noise. It was an immensity of sound."[9]

Although hundreds of local anti-noise ordinances have been enacted in this country, very few have been enforced effectively. The federal government began to take action only a decade ago. Congress asked the newly formed Environmental Protection Agency in 1970 to study the effect of noise on public health. In submitting its report to Congress on Jan. 26, 1972, the agency said noise had a significant effect on about 40 percent of the population. It quoted the World Health Organization as saying that some $4 billion a year was spent in the United States as a result of accidents caused by noise.[10]

The EPA report led to congressional passage of the Noise Control Act of 1972 which authorized the agency to (1) regulate the main sources of noise, including commercial products such as construction equipment, motors and engines, (2) propose aircraft noise standards for implementation by the Federal Aviation Administration, (3) label noisy products, (4) engage in research, technical assistance and dissemination of public information, and (5) coordinate the federal noise control effort.

Quiet Communities Act; Allentown Project

EPA's role in noise control was broadened by the Quiet Communities Act of 1978, which provided more funds for technical assistance to the states and localities. EPA officials, who have been criticized by Congress for running an "ineffective" noise control program,[11] say that the 1978 legislation for the first time gave them sufficient authority to coordinate community and state noise control programs with federal anti-noise activities.

---

[9] H. B. Creswell, writing in the British *Architectural Forum* of December 1958. See "Noise Suppression," *E.R.R.*, 1963 Vol. II, p. 785.
[10] See Congressional Quarterly's 1972 *Almanac*, pp. 979-983.
[11] According to a Senate Environment and Public Works Committee report of May 15, 1979, the EPA noise control program "has been ineffective as a regulatory program to reduce noise" and "enjoys little of EPA's resources or attention." See Congressional Quarterly's 1978 *Almanac*, p. 722.

Measuring Noise

If beauty is in the eye of the beholder, then noise is in the ear of the listener. By definition noise is any sound that is undesired or interferes with hearing. But one's response to loud sounds is conditioned by an individual's psychological makeup and social values — and often by his hearing ability. What may seem loud to one person does not trouble another. A dancer lost in the music of a disco might argue that the sound level in the room was music to his ears — if the dancer's argument could be heard above the din.

In spite of these non-scientific variables, the strength of sound can be measured accurately. The unit of measurement is the decibel. A barely perceptible sound may register only a single decibel. At the other extreme, few people can stand a sound above 140 decibels. The decibel scale is logarithmic. Thus a small increase or decrease in decibels may mean a great change in intensity.

Allentown, Pa., became the first city to receive federal help under the Quiet Communities program. Allentown is an industrial city of 110,000 inhabitants who, according to a 1977 EPA study, ranked noise second only to traffic congestion as the most serious local problem. The survey also indicated that Allentown's residents were willing to pay even more than what is required to implement an effective noise control program.

"Allentown runs the gamut as far as noise problems are concerned, highway, industrial, airport," said Jeffrey Everett, the city's Quiet Communities program coordinator.[12] During the 12-month period that ended in mid-1977, Allentown police received some 1,600 noise-related complaints. EPA engineers studied the local noise problems and in May 1979 the city council passed a noise control ordinance based on their recommendations.

"It is a little early to tell" the total effect of the ordinance, said William Kerr, a noise enforcement officer for the Allentown program. "We might even be getting more complaints now than we did before the ordinance was enacted six months ago. That is because publicity about the new guidelines has interested more people in taking action about excessive noise. We're remedying the problems and we can foresee a dropoff in noise complaints as we get results and people see that those creating noise can be prosecuted."[13]

The EPA began funding similar pilot programs in Spokane, Wash., and Kansas City, Mo., in June 1979. The data gathered from Allentown, Spokane and Kansas City will be used to guide other cities requesting federal help in setting up noise control programs. Publicity about the Allentown program brought a

[12] Quoted in *Nation's Cities*, May 1978, pp. 37-38.
[13] Telephone interview, Feb. 15, 1980.

flood of requests to the EPA's Office of Air, Noise and Radiation from state and local governments. Local jurisdictions also report high citizen interest in noise problems. The city government in San Diego, Calif., reports it has received 35,000 noise complaints in the past five years.

In many instances it appears that the people disturbed by noise complain mostly among themselves until they become aware of an agency or law dealing with the problem. Six months before Chicago put into effect a municipal noise control ordinance in 1971, the city's Environmental Control Office had received only about 150 noise complaints. When the ordinance went into effect, after a city-wide publicity campaign, so many complaints came in that the department accumulated a five-month backlog within days. "Citizen interest in noise control is clearly very high," David Hawkins, EPA assistant administrator for Air, Noise and Radiation, told a House subcommittee last year.[14]

State and Local Cooperative Programs

Fourteen states[15] and the Metropolian Washington (D.C.) Council of Governments have been funded with EPA cooperative agreements under the Quiet Communities program. These states have passed legislation and set up noise control departments with active enforcement programs, or they are in the process of doing so. Administered through 10 regional offices, EPA's state grants are intended to encourage the states to concentrate on providing assistance to individual communities rather than on statewide regulation. About 90 active local noise control programs are in existence.

Under an EPA-backed program called Each Community Helps Others (ECHO), noise control experts from one community advise and assist other communities. For example, noise control authorities from Connecticut have helped set up anti-noise regulations in Iowa, and 16 city employees from Charlotte, N.C., have been trained in the use of sound-measurement equipment by noise control workers in the employ of Daytona Beach, Fla. EPA has provided ECHO financial aid to about 55 local jurisdictions and is aiming eventually to turn financial backing over to the state governments.

There are some 1,000 community noise control ordinances on the books today, up from about 275 in 1972. However, a large number of those laws are "paper laws"; there is little or no

---

[14] Testifying before the House Committee on Interstate and Foreign Commerce's Subcommittee on Transportation and Commerce, March 21, 1979.
[15] California, Colorado, Connecticut, Delaware, Florida, Minnesota, Nebraska, New Jersey, New Mexico, Ohio, Oregon, North Dakota, Utah and Washington.

enforcement power behind them. An effective community noise control program, in EPA's view, should provide for:

Vehicular noise control.

Property line standards to protect people from their neighbors' noise.

Education and public awareness programs.

Noise prevention and abatement considerations in zoning and issuance of building permits.

The 1978 Quiet Communities Act directed EPA to distribute noise control information and education materials. In October 1978, it helped create the National Information Center for Quiet for that purpose. The center, which is run by the non-profit Hearing Educational Aid and Research Foundation, has been receiving a steadily growing number of information requests since its inception 16 months ago. It sponsored a national symposium on environmental noise in Washington in May 1979. Local, state, national and private noise control officials heard speakers explain the latest research on noise control as well as the health effects of noise exposure. Under the center's aegis, Sertoma International, a civic service club that specializes in helping persons with communicative disorders, has set up a pilot program in environmental noise control in St. Louis, Mo.

Noise Standards for Vehicles and Tools

One of EPA's main efforts in the noise control fight is to regulate noise emissions of extra-loud commercial products. In the time-consuming regulatory process, the agency is required first to identify sources of loud noise, then to provide the information on controlling those sources, and finally to regulate the products. The "identified" sources for which regulations have already been promulgated are portable air compressors and medium and heavy trucks.

The noise regulations for trucks, which went into effect in April 1976, call for engine noise levels to be reduced to a maximum of 80 decibels by 1982 and to about 75 decibels by 1985. EPA estimates that some 97 million Americans will feel the benefit in reduced traffic noise when the 1985 truck regulations take effect. "Should these changes in levels seem small," said Charles L. Elkins, deputy assistant administrator of EPA's Office of Noise Abatement and Control, "keep in mind that decibels are calculated on a logarithmic basis and three decibels represents a doubling of the actual noise energy."[16]

Decibel restrictions on crawler tractors and wheel loaders used in construction go into effect in stages between March 1981 and March 1984. The EPA also has proposed standards for "new

---

[16] Quoted in *EPA Journal*, September 1976, p. 5.

truck mounted solid waste compactors" (i.e., garbage trucks), new buses, new motorcycles and new motorcycle exhaust systems, mopeds, truck transport refrigeration units, power lawn mowers and pavement breakers and rock drills. The agency is considering whether to require manufacturers to put noise warning labels on loud machines used around the home, such as radios, household appliances, home workshop tools, power lawn mowers and chain saws.

New York City's Ban; EPA Building Code

New York has a municipal noise control program that is among the strictest in the nation. The New York City Noise Control Code, passed in 1972, "touches directly or indirectly on almost every loud noise in the city," one observer has written, "including those within apartment buildings."[17] Construction work is banned between 6 p.m. and 7 a.m. The same hours apply to music piped onto the street from record shops or discos. The ordinance sets limits on the noise levels of construction equipment, such as air compressors and jackhammers. The law also spells out exactly what types of construction equipment may be used, and requires mufflers for most machines.[18]

New York City's anti-noise law also provides protection from any "unnecessary" noise, regardless of decibel count, if that noise bothers or disturbs a complainant. There are several ways for city residents to fight disturbing noises. The most common is registering a complaint with the city's Division of Air Resources, but New Yorkers may also use the city's Civil Court or the Institute for Mediation and Conflict Resolution. Other alternatives are available not only to New Yorkers, but to anyone affected by unwanted noises. It is possible, for a price, to have an acoustical engineer soundproof an apartment or house. There are also custom-made plastic ear plugs, special draperies and wall panels or partitions to deaden the noise, enclosures for office machines or electronic masking devices that emit pleasing sounds while drowning out unpleasant ones.

For two years, EPA has been working on a model ordinance — one that local jurisdictions could copy when they set noise standards for apartments, condominiums, office buildings, hotels, motels and hospitals. As currently proposed, the model ordinance would require that newly constructed multi-unit buildings contain, among other things, insulated glass, resilient floorings, staggered studs and joists, insulated walls, smooth-running equipment, machine mufflers, and quiet plumbing.

California has a noise insulation standard for new multi-unit

---

[17] Alice DeLury, writing in *New York* magazine, Nov. 6, 1978, p. 103.
[18] See *Nation's Cities,* May 1978, p. 24.

buildings that is similar to the pending EPA code. Under the California law, which took effect in 1974, municipal noise control agencies enforce the construction standards. The law requires, for example, that a one-inch layer of acoustical caulk be added to the bottom and top of all drywalls to shut off air in passageways, thereby cutting down significantly on noise.

"Making improvements in noise can also make a building more energy efficient," said Casey Caccavari, chief of EPA's Division of Air, Noise and Radiation's technical assistance branch. "It would certainly fit in with the Department of Energy's proposed energy standards for the most part. For instance, storm windows not only help keep out the cold but also decrease sound loudness by about one half."[19]

Airport and Airline Noise

ONE OF THE disadvantages of living in many American cities today is exposure to aircraft noise. Big airports across the country have heard complaints from people living nearby. They tell of takeoffs and landings that make conversation impossible, of smoke that pollutes the air overhead, and of the blast that creates vibration and cracked walls.

A Senate committee reported to Congress last year that 6 million people and 900,000 acres of land are exposed to excess aircraft noise levels in this country. The President's Council on Wage and Price Stability has estimated that aircraft noise costs taxpayers who live near airports some $3.5 billion annually in decreased property values. Lawsuits totaling hundreds of millions of dollars are pending today against airports. Potential liabilities due to noise "can be measured in the billion of dollars," the Senate committee reported.[20]

The effort to reduce airport noise is shared by the federal, state and local governments. Responsibility for zoning areas adjacent to airports for land use rests with state and local governments. The federal government, specifically the Federal Aviation Administration (FAA), has the primary responsibility for controlling aviation noise. The government first took action in the late 1950s when jet planes began to be widely used in commercial service for the first time. Responding to a growing volume of complaints about airport noise, Congress first held

[19] Telephone interview, Feb. 15, 1980.
[20] U.S. Senate, Committee on Commerce, Science and Transportation, "Aviation Safety and Noise Abatement Act of 1979," Report, March 29, 1979, p. 3.

hearings on the matter in 1959, but did not give noise abatement authority to the FAA until 1968.

The Federal Aviation Act of 1968 and subsequent amendments empowered the FAA to "prescribe and amend such rules and regulations" as necessary to "provide for the control and abatement of aircraft noise and sonic booms to protect the public health and welfare."[21] The Noise Control Act of 1972 contained a provision directing the EPA to study aircraft and airport noise and to submit regulatory proposals to the FAA. The two agencies have had some problems in agreeing on each other's recommendations. The FAA rejected five of the first seven regulations proposed by the EPA, and the Senate Environment and Public Works Committee said in a report on May 15, 1978, that the environmental agency had been "totally frustrated" in its recommendations on aircraft noise control.

Nevertheless the two agencies have agreed on requirements that some two- and three-engine jet aircraft comply with noise reduction standards by 1981 and others by 1983. Four-engine jets were told to comply by 1985. Airlines were required either to alter or replace the jet engines to meet the new standards. The FAA Office of Environment and Energy estimated in 1977 that 35 percent of the planes then in service were in compliance with the stricter standards.

Effort to Postpone Jet Noise Restrictions

The Senate last year voted to delay the FAA noise control rules for airlines. The bill's backers, including most of the airlines and Sen. Howard W. Cannon, D-Nev., the Senate Commerce Committee chairman, argued that an extension of the noise deadlines would let the airlines convert to quieter equipment in the future without having to make expensive changes in existing equipment to meet intermediate standards. The Airline Transport Association, the airline trade association, estimated that some 1,600 jets in operation would have to be refitted at an average cost of $1 million each.

Airport operators, who are responsible for damages caused by aircraft noise, sided with environmental lobbyists and the Carter administration in opposing a stretched-out timetable. Airport operators from 13 metropolitan areas met with members of Congress in Washington on Nov. 7 to voice their opposition. Robert C. Davidson, deputy director of the Los Angeles International Airport, told the lawmakers that the airport has had to pay some $200 million to settle damage claims from nearby residents and to buy adjoining property to serve as a buffer zone.

The threat of a presidential veto, in addition to House opposition to the Senate bill, prompted House and Senate conferees to

---

[21] Public Law 92-574, 49 USC 1431 (a and b).

The world's first commercial jet passenger plane to fly at super-sonic speeds — faster than sound — brought the question of airport noise to the front pages in the mid-1970s. The governments of France and Britain, beginning in 1962, collaborated to build a supersonic transport (SST), the Concorde. The first scheduled Concorde flights began in Europe in January 1975 but landing rights in New York and Washington were delayed by a series of protests over noise and other environmental factors.

Supersonic flight can create sonic booms, loud thunderclap sounds capable of being heard over a wide area on the ground below. Environmental and citizen groups charged that even the subsonic takeoffs and landings by the Concorde created more racket than other jet airliners did. Their legal challenges reached the Supreme Court but were rejected.

Today, Concorde jets fly into Dallas as well as Washington and New York, but they must adhere to landing and takeoff procedures intended to keep noise within acceptable limits. When flying over the United States they are required to maintain subsonic speeds.

agree to a compromise bill requiring stricter compliance with anti-noise standards than was set out in the original Senate-passed bill.[22] The House on Jan. 31 and the Senate on Feb. 5 accepted the compromise measure and sent it to the White House. President Carter signed it into law on Feb. 19.

As cleared by Congress, the compromise bill exempted two-engine jets with 100 or fewer seats from complying with noise reduction standards until 1988 and two-engine jets with more than 100 seats until 1985. The bill also specified that if the jets are sold after Jan. 1, 1983, they must comply with the present noise standards. A key provision is an authorization of $25 million for noise and land use programs. For the first time, the secretary of transportation would be authorized to grant such funds to municipalities near airports even though the airports were not municipally owned.

Will the increasing — if still limited — national effort to regulate and reduce noise succeed? It is certain that the Envi-

---

[22] A House bill (HR 3942) similar to the original Senate bill (S 413) was approved by the House Public Works Committee on May 15 but was bottled up in the Rules Committee. On Oct. 22, Cannon attached the Senate-passed bill to an unrelated House-passed airport development bill (HR 2440) to force a House-Senate conference on the aircraft noise bill.

ronmental Protection Agency is committed to implementing effective noise control programs. EPA officials concede the obvious: that a great deal remains to be accomplished. No one is guaranteeing a noise-free environment in the foreseeable future, but the results of the expanded governmental anti-noise commitment should provide at least some relief in the next few years in the form of quieter trucks and airplanes.

Selected Bibliography

Books

Bugliarello, George, et al., *The Impact of Noise Pollution*, Pergamon 1976.
Burns, William, *Noise and Man*, Lippincott, 1973.
Goldberg, Philip, *Executive Health*, McGraw-Hill, 1978.
Kavaler, Lucy, *The Dangers of Noise*, Crowell, 1978.
Kryter, Karl D., *The Effects of Noise on Man*, Academic Press, 1970.
May, Daryl N., ed., *Handbook of Noise Assessment*, Van Nostrand Reinhold, 1978.
Nelson, Jon P., *Economic Analysis of Transportation Noise Abatement*, Ballinger, 1978.

Articles

Baldwin, Deborah, "No Noise is Good Noise," *Environmental Action*, July 1, 1978.
DeLury, Alice, "Shhhhhh — Or Else!" *New York*, Nov. 6, 1978.
EPA Journal, selected issues.
"How Noisy is Noise," *CBE Environmental Review*, December 1978.
Lowy, Lyndia, "Airport Environs: Noise-Polluted Land," *Environmental Comment*, March 1979.
Moller, Aage, "How Good are Work Noise Standards?" *New Scientist*, January 1977.
Sarasohn, Judy, "Aircraft Noise Conferees Revise Agreement," *Congressional Quarterly Weekly Report*, Dec. 22, 1979.
Segell, Michael, "The Sounds of Silence: Can Rock & Roll Make You Deaf?" *Rolling Stone*, Feb. 7, 1980.

Reports and Studies

Editorial Research Reports, "Noise Suppression," 1963 Vol. II, p. 785.
United Automobile, Aerospace and Agricultural Implement Workers of America, Social Security Department, "Noise Control: A Worker's Manual," February 1978.
U.S. Environmental Protection Agency, "EPA Noise Control Program: Progress to Date," April 1979.
—— "Noise: A Health Problem," August 1978.
—— "Noise and Its Measurement," February 1977.
—— "Noise Around Our Homes," February 1977.
—— "Noise at Work," February 1977.
U.S. House of Representatives, Committee on Public Works and Transportation, "Aviation Safety and Noise Reduction Act," May 15, 1979.
U.S. Senate, Committee on Commerce, Science and Transportation, "Aviation Safety and Noise Abatement Act of 1979," March 29, 1979.

Toxic Substance Control

by

Marc Leepson

Oct. 13
1 9 7 8

Editor's Note: In October 1980 Congress passed and President Carter signed into law a bill giving the Environmental Protection Agency (EPA) tougher enforcement powers to control "midnight movers," those who illegally dump hazardous wastes. The bill made it a felony for anyone to "knowingly" endanger human life when disposing hazardous wastes. It also allowed EPA to go to court to seek a cleanup order if a hazardous waste could possibly threaten life or the environment.

Also in 1980, Congress passed a bill establishing a $1.6 billion "superfund" to clean up dangerous spills of toxic materials and abandoned waste disposal sites. Part of the fund (87.5 percent) is financed by a tax on oil and chemical companies; the remaining money comes from congressional appropriations.

The regulations governing hazardous waste disposal under the Resource Conservation and Recovery Act of 1976 became effective in November 1980 *(see pp. 106-107)*. As of April 1982, EPA was still promulgating regulations under the Toxic Substances Control Act of 1976. The agency's staff and budget have been cut significantly by the Reagan administration, and many regulations governing the handling of hazardous wastes have been suspended, postponed or revised. Among other things, environmentalists claim that hundreds of millions of dollars collected for the "superfund" are not being used by EPA to clean up abandoned dumps.

TOXIC SUBSTANCE CONTROL

M IDNIGHT MOVER. The phrase evokes images of a late-night disco dancer or someone who skips out on the rent. Actually, a "midnight mover" is a person who disposes of toxic chemical cargoes illegally under cover of darkness. Midnight movers operate in nearly every state of the union. They have dumped toxic substances in sewers, streams, lakes, rivers, oceans, old quarries, forests, fields, trenches and even along roads. Illegal dumping of toxic substances is one manifestation of a much larger national problem: how to prevent the large number of toxic chemicals manufactured and distributed in this country from endangering the health of the American people and poisoning the environment.

Incidents involving poisonous or carcinogenic chemicals have occurred with increasing frequency in the last several years. "The presence of toxic chemicals in our environment is one of the grimmest discoveries of the industrial era," President Carter said last year in an environmental message to Congress. "Toxic substance pollution," Rep. William Brodhead, D-Mich., said recently, "is one of the most pervasive and potentially most devastating health problems today."[1]

Douglas M. Costle, the administrator of the U.S. Environmental Protection Agency, emphasized the seriousness of the situation in a recent article in *The Journal of Commerce*. "The health and environmental hazards stemming from our society's heavy reliance on commercial chemical substances reach into virtually every nook and cranny of modern life," Costle wrote in the Sept. 21, 1978, issue. "Nothing we touch, smell, consume, or otherwise use throughout a given day has not in turn been affected in some way by chemicals."

A widely publicized incident involving toxic substances occurred recently in Love Canal, a small suburb of Niagara Falls, N.Y. Over 200 families were evacuated from the neighborhood last August after New York State Health Commissioner Dr. Robert P. Whalen declared the area unsafe because of the presence of dozens of toxic chemicals, including eight suspected

---

[1] Carter's environmental message to Congress was delivered May 23, 1977. Brodhead testified before the Subcommittee on Consumer Protection and Finance of the House Interstate and Foreign Commerce Committee, March 7, 1978.

cancer-causing substances and two known carcinogens —
benzene and toluene.

Where did the chemicals come from? The answer was immediately apparent. Starting in the 1930s the Hooker Chemicals and Plastics Corp. had disposed of its toxic chemical wastes in metal drums in a deep, open trench — the remains of an aborted 19th century attempt to dig a canal between the Niagara River and Lake Ontario. In 1953, the company turned the site over to the Niagara Falls Board of Education, which filled the ditch and built a school on the site. The school board sold part of the property to developers who built private homes there. Several years ago, heavy rains hit the Niagara Falls area. The drums holding the chemical wastes began to rot and the chemicals made their way to the surface in 1976.

Although there is no absolute proof that the chemicals found in the Love Canal area are directly related to health problems, families in the neighborhood have reported some disturbing medical complaints. Several children were born with birth defects. Four mentally retarded children were born to families on one block. Miscarriages among pregnant women in the neighborhood were 50 percent higher than the national average. Residents also complained of liver ailments, bad eyesight and limb and nervous disorders.

At the time Hooker Chemicals dumped its wastes in the Love Canal ditch there were no state or federal restrictions on hazardous waste disposal. Since no laws were violated, residents are wondering who will pay for damages incurred by the evacuation. The Love Canal Homeowners' Association has hired a Buffalo law firm to consider legal action. "Somebody's responsible here and somebody's going to get sued," said Buffalo attorney Richard J. Lippes of the law firm retained by the citizens' group.[2] Possible defendants include Hooker Chemicals, the city of Niagara Falls, Niagara County, the Board of Education and the state of New York.

Observers in New York estimate that the total cost of evacuating the families and preventing the spread of toxic contaminants could reach $22 million. Work on a drainage and treatment system to prevent further spread of the chemicals — and costing the city of Niagara Falls some $9.2 million — began Oct. 10. The state will spend some $13 million to buy homes for the 237 families that were forced to move. The state also must pay for temporary shelter for the families until new homes are found.

The problems at Love Canal are not unique to that com-

---

[2] Quoted in *Business Week*, Aug. 28, 1978, p. 32.

Where Hazardous Wastes Come From

Industry	Million Metric Tons in 1977
Batteries	0.164
Inorganic Chemicals	3.900
Organic Chemicals, Pesticides and Explosives	11.666
Electroplating	4.053
Paint and Allied Products	0.110
Petroleum Refining	1.841
Pharmaceuticals	0.074
Primary Metals Smelting and Refining	8.973
Textiles Dyeing and Finishing	1.870
Leather Tanning	0.143
Special Machinery	0.153
Electronic Components	0.078
Rubber and Plastics	0.944
Waste Oil Re-refining	0.074
Total	**34.043**

SOURCE: Environmental Protection Agency

munity. There is evidence that other undiscovered leaking disposal sites may exist throughout the nation. "There are ticking time bombs all over" the country, Steffen Plehn, the Environmental Protection Agency (EPA) deputy assistant administrator for solid waste, said recently. "We just don't know how many potential Love Canals there are."[3]

Growth of American Chemical Industry

EPA's Office of Toxic Substances, the primary government regulator of toxic materials *(see box, p. 114),* estimates that there are some 70,000 chemicals manufactured or processed commer-

---

[3] Quoted in *Newsweek,* Aug. 21, 1978, p. 25.

cially in as many as 115,000 establishments across the country. EPA also estimates that about 1,000 new chemical compounds are introduced each year. The government's job is to determine which of these substances is toxic and to protect the environment from these potentially harmful chemicals.

The chemical industry was one of the principal participants in and beneficiaries of the post-World-War II economic and technological boom in the United States. After World War II, the country entered what a government task force termed "a new chemical era."[4] The industry rapidly developed a wide range of new chemicals that were used in making fuels, synthetic fibers, plastics, building materials, fertilizers, pesticides, food additives, detergents, drugs and many other products.

The entire chemical industry, including manufacturers of substances such as plastics, drugs and paints, sold some $113 billion worth of products in 1977, an 11 percent increase over the previous year.[5] By comparison, the industry sold only $13.7 billion worth of chemicals in 1947. Environmentalists, health officials and others have voiced concern about the rapid rate of creation and distribution of new chemical substances. They contend that many new chemicals come into widespread use well before toxicologists are able to determine their effects on health and the environment.

Exposure to Toxic Dangers in Workplace

Nearly 400,000 Americans die from cancer each year, making it the second leading cause of death in the United States. The exact causes of cancer are not known, but the role of environmental carcinogens now is widely accepted. Federal health officials estimate that the proportion of cancer cases brought on by environmental carcinogens is between 55 and 60 percent; other estimates run as high as 85 or 90 percent.[6]

Some scientists and environmentalists contend that the United States is on the verge of a cancer epidemic as the latent effects of exposure to industrial chemicals in the 1940s and 1950s begin to show up as human cancers. "The real fear in my mind," said Gus Speth, a member of the President's Council on Environmental Quality, "is that the post World War II chemical boom could begin to have very serious effects, which, because of the latency period [for cancer] might not begin to show up until 1980. We may begin to see increases in [other] cancers com-

---

[4] U.S. Environmental Protection Agency, et. al., "Environmental Pollution and Cancer and Heart and Lung Disease," First Annual Report to Congress by the Task Force on Environmental Cancer and Heart and Lung Disease, Aug. 7, 1978. p. 4.
[5] Statistics cited in *Chemical and Engineering News*, June 12, 1978, p. 40.
[6] See "Strategies for Controlling Cancer," *E.R.R.*, 1977 Vol. II, p. 579.

parable to [the increase in lung cancer] we saw from smoking."[7]

Scientists at the National Institutes of Health have identified high rates of cancer of the lung, liver and bladder among males in geographic areas with significant employment in the chemical industry, specifically citing Buffalo, Chicago, Cleveland, Detroit and Milwaukee. High incidence of bladder and lung cancer for males in the Northeast also may indicate occupational influences. Secretary of Health, Education and Welfare Joseph A. Califano Jr. recently announced that an as-yet-unreleased government study concluded that at least 20 percent of all future cases of cancer in this country will come from exposure to carcinogens on the job.

Califano singled out asbestos as one of the most toxic carcinogens. Researchers at the Mount Sinai School of Medicine in New York have estimated that 400,000 of the one million Americans who work or have worked with asbestos will die of cancer during the next half century unless better treatment programs are devised.[8] Several studies have indicated that the death rate from a rare form of liver cancer called mesothelioma is three or four times higher than normal among asbestos workers.

In 1974, the B. F. Goodrich Co. disclosed that three workers in its Louisville plant had died of angiosarcoma, a rare but almost invariably fatal form of liver cancer. The disease has been linked to exposure to vinyl chloride — a colorless gas derived from chlorine and petrochemicals and used in the manufacture of plastics. In recent years dozens of U.S. and European workers who suffered prolonged exposure to vinyl chloride are known to have died from angiosarcoma. Other victims did not work in the manufacturing plants, but lived nearby.

Hopewell, Va., once prided itself on being the "chemical capital of the South." But that was before July 1975, when the Life Science Products Co. of Hopewell was forced to shut down. Life Science manufactured a highly toxic pesticide called Kepone. The company operated out of a makeshift plant, a converted gas station near the James River, which flows into the Chesapeake Bay — one of the nation's richest fishing grounds. In the summer of 1975, Virginia health officials found that many of Life Science's employees were suffering from tremors, memory loss, erratic eye movements and chest pains. Over 100 workers had high levels of Kepone in their blood; 28 were subsequently hospitalized. In early 1976 all Kepone production ceased and the plant was dismantled.

---

[7] Quoted in *Congressional Quarterly Weekly Report,* April 22, 1978, p. 960. The period between exposure to carcinogens and the development of cancer — the latency period — ranges from five to 40 years.

[8] See "Job Health and Safety," *E.R.R.,* 1976 Vol. II, p. 953.

Allied Chemical Corp., for which Life Science was the sole supplier of Kepone, was fined $13.2 million in federal court for dumping an estimated 200,000 pounds of Kepone into the James River over a 10-year period. In addition, Allied paid the state of Virginia $5.25 million for cleanup and Kepone research. Allied also paid some $3 million to stricken workers as a result of civil suits. More liability suits are pending.

The lower James River and some of its tributaries have been closed to fishing since December 1975. Researchers continue to find heavy concentrations of Kepone in the James today. The heaviest concentrations have been found 10 miles downstream from Hopewell. Kepone continues to turn up in fish, oysters, crabs and most of the wildlife that feeds on marine organisms in the river. A study by the Environmental Protection Agency indicates that it will cost billions of dollars and take many years before the James is cleansed of Kepone.

Continuing Effects of PBB Contamination

Even when workers are safely shielded from potential carcinogenic or otherwise hazardous chemicals, their highly toxic nature increases the risk of industrial accidents. The worst industrial accident involving toxic chemicals occurred in 1973 when a worker at the Michigan Chemical Co. near Lansing accidentally substituted polybrominated biphenyls (PBBs), a highly toxic fire-retardant, for magnesium oxide in feed prepared for the Michigan Farm Bureau. The mistake was not uncovered until after the feed was distributed to hundreds of Michigan dairy farms. Through the meat, milk and eggs of tens of thousands of farm animals, PBBs passed into the diets of an estimated nine million Michigan residents.

After the mistake was uncovered some 500 farms were quarantined and 23,000 cattle, 150,000 chickens and other farm animals slaughtered. Health researchers conducted a study in November 1976 that compared one thousand Michigan farm residents with a similar group of Wisconsin farm families. The study found that nearly one-third of the Michigan group suffered adverse health effects that could have been caused by PBBs. The researchers, headed by Dr. Irving Selikoff of the Mount Sinai Medical Center, found that the Michigan group had an unusual number of medical problems, including memory loss, muscular weakness, sleep problems and abdominal pain. More studies are under way to determine the exact relationship between the PBBs and the health problems, including possible links to cancer.

Some farmers in Michigan have found that traces of PBB still exist on their property despite intensive clean-up efforts. "It seems like a perpetual circle that can't be broken. I may just have to admit my land is poisoned," dairy farmer Frederic Halbert of Battle Creek said recently.[9] Halbert discovered PBB traces throughout his farm — in the fields, in buildings, and even inside his farmhouse. Halbert recently acquired Wisconsin, Iowa and Indiana-reared cows, but PBB traces were found in the animals because they ate hay grown in PBB-contaminated soil.

Development of Protective Laws

THE PROBLEMS at Love Canal, N.Y., Hopewell, Va., and other areas can be traced directly to improper disposal of toxic wastes. Today most states have laws on the books regulating waste disposal, but few have the resources to adequately police the disposal of hazardous substances. According to a survey in the March 8, 1978, issue of *Chemical Week* magazine, only 13 states — Alaska, California, Illinois, Indiana, Minnesota, New Jersey, New York, North Carolina, Oklahoma, Oregon, Texas, Washington and Wisconsin — have effective laws regulating hazardous waste disposal.

In 1976 Congress passed two laws — the Toxic Substances Control Act (TSCA) and the Resource Conservation and Recovery Act (RCRA) — giving the federal Environmental Protection Agency wide powers in setting restrictions for disposal of toxic waste and other hazardous substances. The two measures supplemented a series of laws passed by Congress during the early 1970s regulating air and water pollution *(see box, p. 107)*.

Ironically, the clean air and water laws, some observers believe, have led to more dumping of toxic wastes on land. The air and water pollution laws mandate the use of high-temperature incinerators and in-house detoxification and waste treatment systems before chemicals can be jettisoned into the air or water. Some companies have decided to dispose of hazardous wastes on land, rather than invest in costly waste detoxification systems.

EPA's Office of Solid Waste has compiled statistics measuring the extent of solid wastes in this country. The office estimates that approximately 10 percent of the 344 million metric tons of solid waste generated by industrial firms each year is hazardous. According to the agency, less than 10 percent of all potentially hazardous waste now is adequately treated or disposed. Most of

[9] Quoted in *The Wall Street Journal*, Aug. 1, 1978.

the hazardous waste — more than 80 percent — is disposed of on land. Only about 2 percent is recovered or recycled. Some 40 percent of potentially hazardous waste material is disposed of or treated away from the site from which it is generated. Private waste handlers operate about 100 legal hazardous waste sites that handle some 7.3 million tons per year. The amount of industrial waste is growing by about 3 percent a year. EPA has found that few chemical manufacturers know exactly how much waste they produce or what percentage of their waste is hazardous.

'76 Laws Restricting Hazardous Substances

The 1976 Resource Conservation and Recovery Act gave the Environmental Protection Agency authority to regulate hazardous wastes from "cradle to grave" — that is, to set up standards covering all facets of hazardous waste handling, from the time the substances leave the factory to their final disposal at approved facilities. When the act is fully implemented, all generators of hazardous wastes will be required to dispose of them at locations meeting minimal federal safety standards.

The Toxic Substances Control Act of 1976 (TSCA) expanded federal regulation of industrial and commercial chemicals and, for the first time, required pre-market testing for potentially dangerous chemicals. The bill directed the Environmental Protection Agency to require that chemical manufacturers test products that pose a risk to human health or the environment. Companies planning to produce a new chemical or to market an existing substance for a new purpose would have to notify the agency 90 days in advance, giving it a chance to hold up marketing while more testing was done or even to ban a chemical in an extreme case.

Both environmentalists and industry officials have criticized EPA efforts to implement the Toxic Substances Control Act and the Resource Conservation and Recovery Act. The chemical industry has complained that EPA efforts under TSCA are overly ambitious and reach beyond the legislative authority. Small manufacturers claim that the pre-market testing procedures mandated by the act will cost them an undue amount of time and money. Environmentalists, on the other hand, claim that the agency has been lax in enforcing the new regulations. In fact, EPA is far behind schedule in implementing both laws.

Under the terms of the Resource Conservation and Recovery Act, regulations governing procedures of hazardous waste disposal were due to have been drawn up by April 1978. Thus far, only three of the seven regulations required under the hazardous waste provisions of the act have been proposed in the Federal Register. EPA officials expect the other four to be proposed early

Federal Regulation of Toxics

There are eight laws that give the federal government control over toxic substances. They are the:

Clean Air Act (as amended), 1970, 1977, administered by the Environmental Protection Agency (EPA); regulates any "air pollutant...which...may cause or contribute to, an increase in mortality or an increase in serious irreversible, or incapacitating reversible, illness."

Water Pollution Control Act (as amended), 1972, 1977, administered by EPA; regulates water "...pollutants which will...cause death, disease, behavioral abnormalities, cancer, genetic mutations, physiological malfunctions...or physical deformations."

Occupational Safety and Health Act, 1970, administered by the Occupational Safety and Health Administration; deals with hazardous substances in the workplace.

Toxic Substances Control Act, 1976, administered by EPA; covers all toxic substances not regulated by other acts; specifically excludes from its jurisdiction foods, drugs, cosmetics and tobacco; regulates substances "...presenting an unreasonable risk of injury to health or the environment."

Federal Food, Drug and Cosmetic Act (as amended) 1958, 1962, administered by the Food and Drug Administration; regulates foods, food additives, other substances or residues in food and substances in cosmetics and drugs.

Federal Insecticide, Fungicide, and Rodenticide Act, administered by EPA.

Safe Drinking Water Act, 1974, administered by EPA.

Resource Conservation and Recovery Act, 1976, administered by EPA; sets standards for generators and transporters of hazardous wastes; allocates permits for treatment, storage or disposal of hazardous waste.

next year. RCRA regulations governing hazardous wastes will not be implemented fully until January 1980 at the earliest. Two public interest groups, the Environmental Defense Fund and Environmental Action, and Illinois Attorney General William J. Scott filed suits against EPA in September for its failure to issue the regulations on time.

EPA is a full year behind schedule in implementing the Toxic Substances Control Act. The agency first must find out what chemicals now are being manufactured and then publish a list of the substances. Part of the reason for the delay in doing this can be traced to inadequate funding and staff. EPA Assistant Administrator for Toxic Substances Steven D. Jellinek told a congressional hearing in April that despite the administrative problems the agency has made "substantial progress in many respects" in carrying out TSCA's mandate. "Once the inventory data are available," Jellinek said, "we will be in a position to systematically select chemical substances and classes of chemical substances for further attention based on their relative production volumes or other factors. In addition, the data will be useful in responding to emergency situations and quickly identifying possible sources of exposure to specific chemical substances."[10]

Illegal Dumping of PCBs and Other Wastes

The Toxic Substances Control Act specifically directed EPA to put an end to the use of polychlorinated biphenyls, PCBs — a group of highly dangerous industrial chemicals long known as one of the most toxic substances ever synthesized. PCBs, which have been in use since 1929, are used as insulating fluids in electrical equipment such as transformers used by utility companies. They also are employed in the production of adhesives, sealants, printing inks, coatings, waxes and many other products. Concerns about PCB pollution have been voiced since 1968, when some 1,000 Japanese citizens suffered severe health problems after ingesting PCB-contaminated rice oil. Japan since has prohibited all production and importation of PCBs.

The U.S. government took its first action against PCBs in 1972. At that time, EPA recommended production curbs, and Monsanto — the sole American PCB producer — voluntarily stopped selling PCBs to those customers who released them into the environment. Later studies showed that salmon, striped bass and other fish in American waterways contained high concentrations of the chemical. Researchers have said that the millions of pounds of PCBs released into the environment will take many years to disappear from fish tissues and bottom sediments.

There is new evidence that PCBs, which have been shown to cause reproductive defects and death in fish, birds and mammals, are spreading up the food chain. Nearly one-third of 1,038 breast milk samples from nursing American women contained measurable amounts of PCBs, according to a national survey conducted for EPA and released on Sept. 14, 1978. Agency researchers theorized that most of the women were exposed to PCBs through their diet. PCBs have caused severe skin and eye irritations and have been linked to reproductive disorders, kidney damage and liver ailments in humans. Large doses have produced liver cancer in laboratory rats.

[10] Testifying before the Subcommittee on Consumer Protection and Finance of the House Interstate and Foreign Commerce Committee, April 26, 1978.

EPA estimates that 440 million pounds of PCBs are in landfills or dispersed throughout the environment. EPA regulations promulgated under TSCA require that all PCB material be specially labeled and disposed of only at EPA-approved waste disposal sites — either chemical-waste landfills or high-temperature incinerators. Generally, solid materials — including power transformers, capacitors, contaminated soil, sludges and drain containers — must be disposed of at waste landfills. Currently, there are four such sites in the nation, located in Grand View, Idaho; Arlington, Ore.; Livingston, Ala.; and Porter, N.Y.

Some observers have expressed concern that EPA's slowness in implementing RCRA and TSCA hazardous waste disposal regulations is contributing to illegal dumping of PCBs and other toxic substances. Illegal waste haulers "operate in nearly every industrialized state," *Chemical Week* magazine reported recently after investigating the situation. "In fact, investigators are convinced that alarming amounts of hazardous chemicals are being poured into rivers, concealed in garbage and buried in municipal landfills, dumped into sewers and ditches, or buried in farmland."[11]

Illegal dumpings have been discovered throughout the country. Six tons of highly toxic chemicals used to make pesticides were dumped into sewers in Louisville, Ky., in March 1977. The city's main sewage treatment plant was forced to close for more than two months as a result. Some workers at the plant were hospitalized with severe eye, nose, throat, lung and skin irritations. At least 100 million gallons of raw sewage a day was dumped into the Ohio River while the treatment plant was closed from March 29, 1977, to June 17, 1977.

A blatant case of illegal dumping occurred recently in North Carolina. Some 33,000 gallons of PCB oil were dumped along 210 miles of secondary roads late in the nighttime hours of July 28. The owner of an Allegheny, N.Y., chemical salvaging firm and his two sons were arrested in the case and face both federal and state charges. The North Carolina Agriculture Commission has warned against "any direct human consumption" of crops within 100 yards of the spills. "This would also apply to pasture and hay for feed," State Agriculture Commissioner James A. Graham said Aug. 25. "In corn for silage, we recommend that the first five or six rows be left and plowed under."[12]

"Cases like the one in North Carolina may become an epidemic before the EPA regulations come into effect," A.

[11] *Chemical Week,* March 1, 1978, p. 25.
[12] Quoted in *The Raleigh News and Observer,* Aug. 26, 1978.

Blakeman Early, legislative director of Environmental Action Inc., a citizens' lobbying group in Washington, D.C., told Editorial Research Reports. "The same things are going to happen with other hazardous wastes. Companies who do not meet EPA disposal regulations are loading up with anything they can find and offering bargain rates."

Public Opposition to Waste Disposal Sites

Most observers say there is a shortage of safe and legal toxic chemical disposal sites. One reason has been citizen opposition to locating such facilities in their backyards. "Everybody wants [a disposal facility] in their state," Jack Lurcott, director of corporative development of Rollins Environmental Services, a waste disposal plant operator, said recently, "but they want it in the opposite corner."[13]

Citizen opposition has forced state and local authorities in some areas to change plans for disposal site locations. Elsewhere, citizen action has affected current waste disposal plant operations. Rollins Environmental Services operates a chemical-waste treatment plant on a 25-acre site in Bridgeport, N.J. Citizens in Bridgeport have expressed concern about the safety of the plant's operations since 1970. A group called "Residents Against Rollins" petitioned the New Jersey Department of Environmental Protection in October 1977 complaining that Rollins was polluting the air and water in the area. In December 1977, an explosion and fire killed six persons and destroyed a chemical tankfarm on the site. Construction of a new tank farm has been halted until Rollins receives approval from state environmental authorities.

The U.S. Occupational Safety and Health Administration's Camden, N.J., office fined Rollins and two of its contractors $45,000 for violations related to the explosion. "We realize the need for such waste-treatment facilities," Mary More, secretary of Residents Against Rollins, said recently, "but we feel the safety of residents, workers and the environment should be of paramount importance. If Rollins does reopen its operations, we think the state should inspect the plant more frequently and run tests.... Also, we would like to have an independent laboratory test the air and water in the area of the plant."[14]

In Wilsonville, Ill., some 40 miles northeast of St. Louis, citizen opposition led to a court order closing a nearby chemical waste disposal facility. The plant in question is a 130-acre facility called Earthline, owned by SCA Services, Inc. of Boston, Mass. Earthline began operations in Wilsonville in November

---

[13] Quoted in *The Wall Street Journal*, May 1, 1978.
[14] Quoted in *Chemical Engineering*, May 22, 1978, p. 56.

1976. In April 1977, EPA directed that Earthline receive thousands of pounds of PCB-contaminated soil from a farm in Ditmar, Mo. That action brought sharp reaction from Wilsonville residents.

Illinois state officials eventually became involved. The state attorney general's office sued to have the site closed. The state claimed that the plant was built on an abandoned coal mine whose vertical cracks allowed toxics to seep into ground water supplies. Circuit Court Judge John Russell in Macoupin County, Ill., agreed and ordered the plant to close. SCA has appealed the ruling.

EPA officials are worried about the consequences of the Wilsonville plant closing and other movements against toxic disposal sites across the nation. "A very serious problem is developing," Chuck Grigalauski, an enforcement officer with the Chicago EPA office, said after Judge Russell's order. "The closing of the Earthline Corp. site in Wilsonville has national ramifications. If that site closes, we don't know where a lot of industries are going to take their hazardous wastes. It could mean that a lot more of that stuff will be dumped down sewers and on abandoned farms."[15]

Concern About Pesticide Usage

PESTICIDES and herbicides are among the most toxic substances produced by the chemical industry. "Pesticides kill insects by design," author Erik P. Eckholm wrote recently, "and poisonings of some people who apply or work amid them is part of an almost inevitable pattern."[16] The first synthetic pesticide that proved vastly more effective than earlier poisons found in nature — DDT — was developed during World War II. Following the war, the chemical pesticide and herbicide industry grew rapidly. Between 1950 and 1963, sales value of pesticides at the manufacturers' level tripled. Today, the industry accounts for some $8 billion worth of sales. Farmers have credited the use of pesticides and herbicides with increasing yields and keeping labor costs down. Little was known about the health or environmental effects of pesticides and there was no organized, vocal opposition to the chemicals until the 1960s.

In 1962 *Silent Spring* by Rachel Carson was published, in-

[15] Quoted in The *Louisville Courier Journal*, Sept. 5, 1978.

[16] Erik P. Eckholm, *The Picture of Health: Environmental Sources of Disease* (1977), p. 165.

troducing a frightening note of urgency into ther risks associated with pesticide use. Carson, a noted biologist, pictured the advent of a silent — that is, lifeless — spring caused by long-continued and spreading chemical contamination of air, soil, water, vegetation and animal life. Her conclusions were denounced and ridiculed by the pesticide industry. But many Americans became concerned about the potential effects of pesticides.

Debate Over Safety of Defoliant 2,4,5-T

DDT was banned by the EPA in 1972 when it was discovered that the pesticide tended to accumulate in the environment. Eleven other pesticides[17] cited by Carson as potentially hazardous also have been banned, regulated or phased out. Currently there are thousands of pesticides and herbicides in widespread use around the world. No one believes that all of them pose dangers to humans or the environment. But questions about the toxic effects of a number of widely used herbicides and pesticides have surfaced in recent years. One such chemical is 2,4,5-T, which contains a substance called dioxin — "one of the most toxic substances known to man."[18] The chemical 2,4,5-T is a primary ingredient in Agent Orange, the defoliant used to destroy some 5 million acres of jungle in Vietnam. In this country, some 12 million pounds of 2,4,5-T are manufactured each year and used in a less toxic form to clear forests of unwanted vegetation to facilitate timber production.

Worldwide attention was focused on 2,4,5-T two years ago when a chemical reactor producing the substance exploded at each year and used in a less toxic form to clear forests of unwanted vegetation to facilitate tree growth and timber production. Seveso and residents soon experienced nausea, dizziness, headaches, diarrhea and skin irritations. After health authorities identified dioxins among the falling debris, Seveso's 400 residents were evacuated. Produce and livestock grown in the town were banned from market. To date, scientists have not verified a positive link between dioxin and the ailments reported in Seveso. And no deaths have occurred that can be directly tied to dioxin poisoning. But many are concerned about the latent effects of the chemical.

Environmentalists in this country have petitioned EPA to have 2,4,5-T banned on the ground that it is highly toxic to humans, fish and wildlife and that it can cause cancer and birth defects. They cite one study that found traces of dioxin in the milk of lactating mothers in areas of Oregon and Texas where 2,4,5-T is extensively sprayed. Another study, by the Oregon

---

[17] Malation, parathion, dieldrin, aldrin, endrin, chlordane, heptachlor, toxaphene, lindane, benxene hexachloride and 2-4-D.
[18] Thomas Whiteside, "Contaminated," *The New Yorker,* Sept. 4, 1978, p. 35.

Regional Primate Research Center, showed relatively high doses of dioxin in pregnant rhesus monkeys caused miscarriages and one death. Timber companies and the U.S. Forest Service, on the other hand, say that 2,4,5-T is being used in a safe manner and is not dangerous. They also maintain that a ban would result in excessive costs for manual labor in clearing out brush in forest regions.

Assistant Agriculture Department Secretary M. Rupert Cutler, on Aug. 11, 1978, banned the use of 2,4,5-T in the Rogue River National Forests of Oregon and California. Cutler also ruled that 2,4,5-T could not be sprayed within a quarter of a mile of streams on national forest land and within one mile of permanent residences. Less than a month later, however, Cutler — under pressure from timber interests — announced that he would allow spraying within 200 feet of streams. Cutler also said he was reconsidering the ban in the Rogue River National Forest.

A report prepared for the Council for Agricultural Science and Technology,[19] an organization of 25 societies with headquarters in Ames, Iowa, maintains that 2,4,5-T and another related herbicide, Silvex, contain only minute portions of dioxins. "There just isn't enough [dioxin] in [2,4,5-T] to have any toxicological significance," said William B. Seward, a spokesman for Dow Chemical, the largest U.S. manufacturer of 2,4,5-T.[20]

Proposed Solutions to Disposal Problems

All observers of the hazardous chemical problem agree that protecting human health and the environment from the effects of chemical toxics is an extremely complex proposition. The main reason is the vast number of chemicals that touch the everyday lives of nearly all Americans. Only a small percentage of these chemicals pose threats to man and the environment, but total effective safeguarding against toxics probably never will be accomplished. "It just boggles the mind to think how little is known," said Carroll Bastion, a toxic substances expert for the President's Council on Environmental Quality. "There will never be a way to reduce the hazards of toxic substances to zero even if we return to a much simpler society."[21]

Some observers contend that the full implementation of the Resource Conservation and Recovery Act and the Toxic Substances Control Act will help ease the problem. Others have suggested economic incentives to force the chemical industry to cut down on the manufacture of suspected hazardous sub-

[19] "The Phenoxy Herbicides," 2nd ed., Council for Agricultural Science and Technology, Report No. 77, August 1978.
[20] Quoted in *The Christian Science Monitor*, Sept. 29, 1976.
[21] Quoted in *The Wall Street Journal*, May 9, 1978.

Federal Fight Against Toxics

Environmental Protection Agency administers federal environmental policies, research and regulations. Office of Toxic Substances studies and makes recommendations for regulation of toxic chemicals. Office of Solid Waste administers programs on resource conservation and solid waste management, including hazardous waste materials.

National Cancer Institute of the National Institutes of Health operates a large number of programs aimed at identifying environmental carcinogens, quantifying the relationship between these carcinogens and cancer incidence, and prevention of cancer incidence through educational and other programs.

National Heart, Lung and Blood Institute of National Institutes of Health supports research into causes, prevention and treatment of diseases of the heart and lungs. Has various programs aimed at determining the relationship between these diseases and environmental pollutant agents.

National Institute for Occupational Safety and Health (NIOSH) supports research to assess interaction between chemical and physical agents, and to develop new monitoring techniques, analytical methods and methods of diagnosing and preventing specific occupational diseases.

National Institute of Environmental Health Sciences of National Institutes of Health conducts research on identifying environmental disease agents and studying health hazards and epidemiology. Emphasizes development of environmental health science resources through grants and training programs.

National Center for Health Statistics of U.S. Department of Health, Education and Welfare compiles general health statistics. Produces data on disease incidence that frequently provide the basis for research carried out to determine and quantify the relationships between disease and environmental pollutant agents.

Center for Disease Control works with NIOSH to help under stand and prevent environmentally related disease in occupational contexts.

National Center for Toxicological Research of Food and Drug Administration conducts research on biological effects of toxic substances in the environment; evaluates effects of food additives, environmental pollutants and other toxic chemicals on man.

stances. A toxic tax levied on suspicious substances while research goes on to determine their hazardous potential is one suggestion. The tax would be similar to the excise tax now levied on cigarettes and liquor. The proceeds of the tax would go to fund cancer research or research on toxics. The higher prices of the taxed substances could cut sales and perhaps induce manufacturers to stop or limit production of hazardous substances or turn to non-hazardous alternatives.

The problem of the shortage of safe hazardous substances disposal sites, most observers agree, is going to get worse before there is any improvement. "The ultimate solution is the minimization of wastes to land disposals," A. Blakeman Early of Environmental Action told Editorial Research Reports. "One way to accomplish that would be to make processing changes geared toward recycling within the chemical production process or producing wastes that are recyclable." Chemical industry scientists are working on processes for treating and reclaiming materials from chemical wastes. But industry officials say it will be years before industry-wide recycling technology will cut the amount of wastes significantly. Many of the nation's leading chemical companies, including Dow, Monsanto, and Du Pont, have greatly increased toxicological laboratory facilities and have hired more toxicologists to study alternative waste-disposal methods for toxic substances.

The final answer to the problem may be that Americans will have to make drastic changes in their lifestyles. Since dozens of chemicals thought to be hazardous play a role in the way Americans live and work today, any changes will be extremely difficult to bring about. Some say significant change will occur only in reaction to an environmental or health disaster directly attributable to a widely used chemical.

"We look back on the Middle Ages, and we say 'No wonder they had bubonic plague — they used to throw their garbage in the streets,' " EPA administrator Costel said recently. "Now I just hope that in the year 2025 my grandchildren don't look back on this generation and say, 'No wonder they had problems — look at all the chemicals just carelessly introduced into the environment, uncontrolled.' "[22] No one is predicting the imminent coming of bubonic plague or anything similar. But with the number of potentially hazardous substances increasing every year, the potential for incidents such as those in Love Canal, N.Y., Hopewell, Va., Seveso, Italy, and elsewhere increases daily.

---

[22] Quoted in *Newsweek*, Aug. 21, 1978, p. 28.

Selected Bibliography

Books

Ashford, Nicholas, *Crisis in the Workplace: Occupational Health and Safety,* MIT Press, 1976.

Brown, Lester R., *The Twenty-Ninth Day: Accommodating Human Needs and Numbers to the Earth's Resources,* Norton, 1978.

Eckholm, Erik P., *The Picture of Health: Environmental Sources of Disease,* Norton, 1977.

McRae, Alexander and Leslie Whelchel, eds., *Toxic Substances Control Sources Book,* Aspen Systems Corporation, 1978.

Articles

"Aftermatch of Two Environmental Shocks, *U.S. News & World Report,* Feb. 13, 1978.

Chemical Week, selected issues.

Commoner, Barry, "The Promise and Perils of Petrochemicals," *The New York Times Magazine,* Sept. 25, 1977.

Culliton, Barbara J., "Toxic Substances Legislation," *Science,* Sept. 29, 1978.

Gwynne, Peter, et al., "The Chemicals Around Us," *Newsweek,* Aug. 21, 1978.

Pelham, Ann, "Government Tackles Tricky Question of How to Regulate Carcinogens," *Congressional Quarterly Weekly Report,* April 22, 1978.

Reddig, William, "Industry's Preemptive Strike Against Cancer," *Fortune,* Feb. 13, 1978.

Scott, Rachel, "The Political Hazards of Cancer Research," *Environmental Action,* June 4, 1977.

Slesin, Louis, "Regulating Chemicals Under TOSCA," *Environment,* March 1978.

Speth, Gus, "The Toxic Environment Is Everybody's Business," *The Center Magazine,* May-June 1978.

"Who Will be Liable for Toxic Dumping?" *Business Week,* Aug. 28, 1978.

Wynder, Ernst L. and Gio B. Gori, "Contribution of the Environment to Cancer Incidence: An Epidemiologic Exercise," *Journal of the National Cancer Institute,* April 1977.

Zwerdling, Daniel, "Can U.S. Farmers Kick the Petrochemical Habit?" *New Times,* May 29, 1978.

Reports and Studies

Editorial Research Reports, "Strategies for Controlling Cancer," 1977 Vol. II, p. 579; "Job Health and Safety," 1976 Vol. II, p. 951; "Ozone Controversy," 1976 Vol. I, p. 207; "Pesticide Control," 1964 Vol. I, p. 363.

Environmental Action Foundation, "Hazardous Wastes: Hidden Danger," 1978.

Executive Office of the President, Council on Environmental Quality, "Environmental Quality-1977: The Eighth Annual Report of the Council on Environmental Quality," December 1977.

U.S. General Accounting Office, "Waste Disposal Practices — A Threat to Health and the Nation's Water Supply," June 16, 1978.

Protecting Endangered Wildlife

by

Marc Leepson

Editor's Note: Congress passed a bill on Oct. 15, 1977, establishing a seven-member board that can allow construction of dams and other projects even if they threatened the existence of a species protected by the 1973 Endangered Species Act. The panel's first act was to refuse to exempt the Tennessee Valley Authority's Tellico Dam because its construction would destroy the habitat of an endangered three-inch fish, the snail darter. But in 1979, Congress exempted the Tellico Dam from the law in an amendment attached to an appropriations bill.

The Endangered Species Act is up for reauthorization in 1982 and the administration may try to change the law to make it easier for developers to use lands designated as "critical habitats" of endangered species. Since President Reagan came into office, no new species have been added to the government's official endangered list. The listing process has been held up while the Office of Endangered Species assesses the economic effects of its regulations, as a result of the president's order that all proposed regulations be similarly reviewed. The latest government statistics, released in October 1980, showed that in this country 228 species — including 35 mammals, 69 birds, 46 fishes, 26 reptiles and 8 amphibians — fell into the endangered category.

PROTECTING ENDANGERED WILDLIFE

O NE OF THE consequences of the world's expanding population[1] is the further endangerment of the 250,000 species of animals and plants found on earth. Until this century, the hunting of animals for skins and food was mankind's principal threat to wildlife. Today, however, it is the influx of civilization that is the chief source of danger to wildlife in the United States and around the world.

"The expansion of cities, construction of highways and electric power dams, the use of poisonous chemicals in agriculture and industry, dumping of heavy metals in water, harvesting and conversion of forests, the increase in leisure activities that sends millions of people into wildlife territory...impose heavy pressures" on the world's wildlife, an environmentalist has written.[2] Every new highway, shopping mall or suburban housing development diminishes the amount of open land supporting birds and animals. Pollution of the world's waterways takes a heavy toll of fish and other marine life. Use of pesticides on crops and trees brings death to millions of birds and animals as well as to insects.

The latest statistics from the Interior Department's Fish and Wildlife Service (FWS), the agency that keeps track of U.S. and foreign endangered species, show that in this country alone, no fewer than 181 species—including 36 mammals, 68 birds, 30 fishes, 10 reptiles and 4 amphibians—fall into the endangered species category.[3] The Endangered Species Act of 1973 (see p. 129) defined an endangered species as one "which is in danger of extinction throughout all or a significant portion of its range." The act also set up another category of protected animals, known as "threatened" species, of which there were 18 in the United States as of Sept. 12, 1977. A threatened species is defined as one "which is likely to become an endangered species within the foreseeable future throughout all or a significant portion of its range."

This past year at least half a dozen bills have been introduced in Congress or drafted to revise the 1973 law or make exceptions

---

[1] Most experts predict the world's population will double to about eight billion sometime during the first two decades of the next century.

[2] Michael Frome, *Battle for the Wilderness* (1975), p. 66.

[3] The official U.S. endangered species list contained only 78 species 10 years ago. See "Wildlife Preservation," *E.R.R.*, 1967 Vol. I, p. 341. The current listing of 181 species includes four plants.

to it. The target of the proposed amendments is a provision of the act which directs the Secretary of the Interior to insure that federal construction projects do not interfere with the lives of threatened or endangered species. Opponents of this provision argue that human factors—such as the economic condition of the area, the number of jobs which would be produced, etc. — should be given equal consideration *(see p. 130)*.

The FWS's Office of Endangered Species is responsible for determining which species go on the endangered and threatened lists. There are 10 steps that a species must go through—what an observer has called a "formidable obstacle course"[4]—before it is officially declared threatened or endangered. The first step consists of formal notification that a species appears in danger and that its status is being reviewed by the Fish and Wildlife Service. Those with information that could help determine that species' status are publicly invited to comment.

The minimum amount of time needed to certify a species is 36 days.[5] Once a species is listed as endangered, it is illegal for anyone "to harass, harm, pursue, hunt, shoot, wound, kill, trap, capture, or collect [it] or to attempt to engage in any such conduct." Land areas found to support endangered species are categorized as "critical habitats," and are protected by the government. There currently are seven existing critical habitats; 45 more have been proposed. President Carter has pledged to speed up the process of identifying and protecting endangered species. On May 23, he asked the Secretaries of Interior and Commerce to devise methods to hasten the identification process.

U.S. System of National Wildlife Refuges

The concept of wildlife habitats was not new with the 1973 Endangered Species Act. The Fish and Wildlife Service also administers the National Wildlife Refuge System, which contains 387 separate wildlife preserves, covers some 34 million acres, and—in the words of FWS Director Lynn A. Greenwalt—"provides habitat resources for virtually every species of wildlife found in North America."[6] The refuges are set up primarily to protect waterfowl. Some 274 are set aside for ducks alone. Others, which exist in 49 states, Puerto Rico, the Virgin Islands and American Samoa, provide havens for such varied animals as antelopes, big horn sheep, deer, caribou and

---

[4] Janet L. Hopson, "A Plea for a Mundane Mollusk," *The New York Times Magazine*, Nov. 14, 1976, p. 58.

[5] One of the latest status reviews was announced Aug. 10, 1977. Ten species of amphibians (toads, frogs and salamanders) found in widely scattered parts of the country were proposed for the endangered list.

[6] Lynn A. Greenwalt, "A Place for Wildlife to Live," *American Forests*, December 1976, p. 16.

Endangered Wildlife Species

	U.S.	Foreign
Mammals	36	227
Birds	68	144
Amphibians and Reptiles	14	55
Fish	30	10

ATKINSON

SOURCE: U.S. Fish and Wildlife Service

wild turkeys. About 19 million acres of the wildlife refuge system are in Alaska.[7]

The National Wildlife Refuge System, like many other federal government programs, has been plagued by financial problems. Greenwalt has written that the system "has never been able to provide the optimum level of total public benefits...of which it is capable" because of insufficient funding."[8] The following table illustrates the system's field management funding over the last 20 years.

Year	Money allocation (millions)	Permanent Employees	Number of Refuges
1957	$ 5.4	497	270
1968	10.5	930	331
1976	24.9	835	367

[7] Alaska, with 375 million acres, is larger than the next three largest states combined. Most of the state is wilderness, with only 100,000 acres taken up by cities, towns, villages, roads and other marks of human activity. See "Alaskan Development," *E.R.R.*, 1976 Vol. II, p. 927.

[8] Greenwalt, *op. cit.*, p. 19.

In the past decade the system's staff has dropped while the number of refuges has risen. And, even though the budget has risen, inflation and expansion have eroded much of the increase. Because of the funding situation, money for maintenance and upkeep and for purchases of new refuges has been in short supply. The funding problem is especially serious because additional endangered species are being discovered every year and more refuges will be needed in the future.

A number of states have set aside land for wildlife conservation. Fiscal problems have arisen in the states as well. Many states are hard-pressed to allocate money for wildlife conservation. The director of Colorado's Division of Wildlife, Jack R. Grieb, has said that his agency does not receive enough funds to determine adequately what species to add to the state's endangered list. The problem is especially apparent in his agency's attempt to protect non-game species. The state legislature authorized $125,000 to study non-game species for fiscal year 1976. Grieb had asked for $1-million.

Growing Interest in Non-Game Animals

Within the last 10 years there has been what has been termed[9] a "growing trend" to include non-game birds and mammals in wildlife conservation legislation. State wildlife agencies are set up mainly to watch over game species, but many of them have started programs to protect non-game animals. For example, the New Jersey state legislature appropriated $100,000 in 1973 to finance a study of how best to protect such endangered non-game species as the blue-spotted salamander, bog turtle, osprey and bald eagle. Last year, New Jersey state wildlife officials successfully reintroduced the peregrine falcon to the state. Ten chicks were transferred from Cornell University in upstate New York, and fed and protected until they could fly. They then were sent on their own, thus becoming the first of their species to be seen in New Jersey since 1957.

Dozens of other projects have been undertaken by various state wildlife agencies with non-game species. These include prairie chickens, lynx, timber wolves, ospreys, spruce grouse, hawks and owls in Michigan, pine martins in Wisconsin, masked bobwhites in Arizona and brown pelicans in Florida. As with other programs, money is a problem. "A large majority of state wildlife agencies," Charles H. Callison of the National Audubon Society said recently, "are ready to extend research and management operations to non-game species. The key problem is funding."[10]

---

[9] By George Laycock, writing in *Audubon,* May 1977, p. 128.

[10] Quoted by George Laycock, p. 131.

Fees for hunting licenses are used in part to oversee the preservation of hunted animals. But it has been difficult to find revenues specifically for the protection of non-game animals. Some states have introduced specialized fund-raising programs to try to get money from the general public, since there is no one group that deals directly with non-game species. Revenue from the sale of personalized license plates in California goes toward the purchase of refuges for endangered non-game species in that state. A similar plan has been approved in the state of Washington. There are programs in which decals and stamps are sold for the benefit of non-game animals in Colorado, Ohio, Michigan and New Hampshire.

So far, the California plan is the only non-game preservation program that has had any measure of success. Sen. Gary Hart (D Colo.) introduced a bill in Congress this year to encourage states to establish such programs. Under the bill, states would develop their own programs for research, habitat location, and law enforcement affecting non-game animals. If a state proposal is approved by the Fish and Wildlife Service, it would then become eligible for federal funds. The Hart bill, as originally drafted, planned to finance the non-game conservation programs through a tax on hiking gear, such as backpacks and lightweight stoves. But Hart was inundated with protests from hikers, manufacturers and congressional tax specialists, and he eventually dropped the tax provision from his bill.

Efforts to Help Whooping Cranes Survive

The whooping crane, the tallest of all birds in North America, has been a widely publicized endangered species for over 50 years. One-hundred and twenty were counted in mid-summer in the wild and in captivity, the most since records were first kept in the 1930s. But the final 1977 count won't be known until the wild flocks make their perilous fall migration southward from Canada to the U.S. Gulf Coast. These snowy white birds, which reach five feet in height, never were very numerous. Each family requires a large area, both for its wintering ground and for its nesting and breeding ground in the summer. But civilization's encroachment during the 20th century reduced the range of the whoopers. As the range shrank, and as some of the birds were shot by hunters, the population diminished.

In 1938 the first refuge for whooping cranes was established in Texas, at Aransas Bay on the Gulf Coast. Since then, the number of birds has increased gradually, although there have been some setbacks. The whooper population at the Aransas National Wildlife Refuge reached a low point of 15 in the winter of 1941-42. Today most experts believe that careful conservation methods have been responsible for the whooping crane's victory in its battle to survive. "The crane has gotten to the point now where we can almost relax," said Cameron Kepler, who is in charge of whoopers at the Patuxent Wildlife Center in Laurel, Md.[11]

The 69 whoopers in the main North American flock include 12 that were hatched in 1976. That group nests at Wood Buffalo National Park in Canada and then migrates more than 2,000 miles in September after their young—who are hatched in late June—are ready to fly. Migration is completed in December when the whoopers return to rest at Aransas Bay. American and Canadian wildlife authorities set up a plan two years ago to establish a second flock at Grays Lake National Wildlife Refuge in Idaho. Eggs were removed from the first flock and placed in the nests of sandhill cranes. Five of the whoopers born in Idaho have survived. The second flock's ultimate fate will be decided when the whoopers mature in five or six years and are ready to produce offspring.

U.S. Wildlife Protection Laws

EVEN THOUGH the wildlife conservation movement has been in evidence for over a century in this country, it was not until 1973 that Congress passed a law that imposed criminal penalties for taking an endangered species of animal. The Endangered Species Act of 1973 mandates up to one year in jail and a fine of not more than $20,000 for the killing or capturing of any of the 181 U.S. endangered species. Laws regulating wildlife have changed significantly since the first ones were enacted by Congress in the 19th century. The early laws concentrated on specific game animals. Such legislation set up hunting seasons and restricted the amount and size of game that could be killed. Federal regulation of wildlife continued throughout this century and the laws became more inclusive, moving away from specific classes of animals.

Several animal species became extinct before the 20th century. The last dodo, a member of the pigeon family that was native to the island of Mauritius, was killed in 1693. The great auk, a large flightless bird like the dodo, once was found in widely separated areas of the North Atlantic region from America to Europe. It was hunted for its feathers and the last pair was killed in 1844.

---

[11] Quoted in *Potomac* magazine of *The Washington Post*, May 2, 1976, p. 54.

Return of the Alligator

New animal species are being added to the official U.S. endangered list regularly. But every so often a species is taken off the endangered list—not because it is extinct, but because conservation programs succeeded in adding significantly to its population.

One such species is the American alligator. Alligators were protected by state laws in Florida, Louisiana, the Carolinas, Alabama, Mississippi, Arkansas and Texas during the 1960s because their numbers were diminishing rapidly due to large-scale killings of the reptiles for hides. But the state laws were widely evaded by poachers.

The 1969 Endangered Species Act has been credited with sparking the alligator's comeback. That law made it a federal crime to traffic in alligator products and eliminated a good deal of illicit killing. The alligator population reached about one million by the end of 1976 and the next month the U.S. Fish and Wildlife Service transferred most species from the endangered to the threatened list. State and federal wildlife agency employees will now be able to kill or relocate animals that cause "nuisances."

About 10,000 complaints a year are received by the Florida Game and Fresh Water Fish Commission, whose staff spends around a third of its time on alligators. The biggest problem is caused when full-grown alligators range far from the swamps and terrorize suburban dwellers.

Even though there was a scattering of local and state laws regulating some types of hunting, such regulations rarely were enforced before 1900. Wild game was plentiful in 19th-century America. But as the U.S. population moved westward and grew, the demand for food and pelts rose as well. So insatiable was the demand for fur garments that the beaver was in danger of extinction.

Near Extinction of the American Buffalo

It is believed that buffalo herds constituted the biggest aggregation of land animals anywhere on earth when the white man first arrived in North America. Wildlife experts estimate that at least 60 million buffaloes roamed the continent until well into the 19th century. Systematic hunting of the buffalo began around 1825, but the real devastation came with the construction of the Union Pacific Railroad in the 1860s. What author Dee Brown has called "an army of hide hunters"[12] conducted a wholesale slaughter of the buffalo and came close to exterminating them.

The number killed has been estimated to be 2.5 million a year during the height of the slaughter, from 1870 to 1875. One

---

[12] Dee Brown, *I Hear that Lonesome Whistle Blow* (1977), p. 259.

goal of the buffalo hunters was to starve and force the Plains Indians into submission by eliminating their basic food, the main source of their shelter and clothing and their major folk hero and religious symbol. By 1883, only one buffalo herd, consisting of around 10,000 animals, was left in the United States. And it, too, was nearly exterminated. A census taken in 1889 showed a total buffalo population of 541, made up of several small groups of animals. Today, a few thousand buffalo remain, protected by laws, on western ranges.

At one time the passenger pigeon also was found in plentiful numbers in the United States. Tens of millions of the birds were slaughtered in the 1860s and 1870s for food. By the early 1900s, they were extinct—except for a few pairs in the Cincinnati Zoological Gardens. The last known passenger pigeon died in September 1914. Water pollution is thought to have been the reason for the demise of the harelip sucker fish, which became extinct in 1893. Since then, 11 other U.S. fish species and four subspecies have disappeared.

Moves Toward Comprehensive Legislation

There were only several minor pieces of federal wildlife legislation in the 19th century. All were limited to specific species. These laws included an 1868 act prohibiting the killing of some fur-bearing animals in and around Alaska, an 1887 measure that regulated the importation of mackerel and an 1894 law prohibiting hunting of wildlife in Yellowstone National Park. The basis for the government's power to regulate the nation's wildlife came from an 1842 Supreme Court ruling.[13] The court ruled for the first time in that case that wildlife were not the property of any individual, but were owned by all the people and therefore subject to government regulation.

The Lacey Act, passed in 1900, prohibited the killing of game for profit. Called a "very cautious first step in the field of federal wildlife regulation,"[14] the Lacey Act prohibited interstate transportation of wildlife killed in violation of state laws. It thereby established the federal government as the enforcer of state game laws through its control over interstate commerce. Not until the 1930s did any comprehensive laws take effect widening the government's role in wildlife protection and preservation. The first federal wildlife refuge was established on Pelican Island, off the Florida coast, by President Theodore Roosevelt in 1903. Roosevelt, though also known as a big-game hunter, supported the newly established Audubon Society,[15] which was concerned

---

[13] *Martin v. Waddell*, 41 U.S. (16 Pet.) 234.

[14] Michael J. Bean, "The Evolution of National Wildlife Law," published by the Council on Environmental Quality, p. 20. The act was named for Rep. John F. Lacey (R Iowa).

[15] Formed in 1901 as the National Association of Audubon Societies for the Protection of Wild Birds and Animals. It was named for the noted ornithologist John J. Audubon.

Bald Eagle: Vanishing National Symbol

The U.S. Fish and Wildlife Service has proposed that the northern bald eagle—the symbol of the nation for the past 200 years—be added to the endangered species list in 43 states and to the threatened list in five others. "It is ironic...," FWS Associate Director Keith M. Schriener has said, "that...the living embodiment of the spirit of America is in such a predicament."

That proposal currently is in the final stages of the review process. It pertains to all bald eagles that live north of the 40th parallel, excluding Alaska. The southern bald eagle—identical to the northern species except that it is slightly smaller—has been on the endangered list since 1967. And all bald eagles come under the Bald Eagle Protection Act of 1940, which imposes up to a one-year prison sentence and a $5,000 fine for killing one.

The FWS estimates that there are only 750 to 1,000 nesting pairs of southern bald eagles. They are found in coastal areas from New Jersey to Texas, in the lower Mississippi River valley from Arkansas and Tennessee southward, and throughout the southern states and in California. Most of the northern eagles, perhaps 40,-000 in all, are found in Alaska.

Civilization's march has been the main cause of the threat to the bald eagle. Loss of their natural habitat is felt most acutely in the lower Great Lakes region, and in New York and New England. It is thought that there are not more than 100 bald eagles left in the entire northeastern United States. Man's transgressions have caused harm in other ways. Pesticides have contaminated many of the birds, to the extent that some females cannot produce eggs with shells thick enough to allow the chicks to be hatched. And illegal shooting, the FWS says, remains "the leading cause of premature death" of young and adult bald eagles.

with the impact of America's expanding population on the natural habitats of animals.

Establishment of the National Park Service in 1916 was another step forward in the wildlife preservation movement. Hunting was banned on all land administered by the service. Legislation which aided the bird-refuge movement included (1) a 1918 treaty between the United States and Canada for protection of migratory birds; (2) the Norbeck-Andersen Migratory Bird Conservation Act of 1929, which provided for development of a system of refuges; and (3) the 1934 Migratory Bird Hunting Stamp Act, which required all hunters over 16 years of age to purchase a $1 federal waterfowl stamp (the "duck stamp") before hunting any migratory waterfowl anywhere in the country. Proceeds from the stamps were used to finance purchases of new waterfowl refuge areas.

The 1934 Fish and Wildlife Coordination Act was the first by Congress limiting development on land owned by the federal government. It authorized federal agencies controlling suitable land and water resources to make portions available to two government agencies—the Commerce Department's Bureau of Fisheries and the Agriculture Department's Bureau of Biological Survey—for use as fish and wildlife management and refuge areas. Those bureaus were transferred to the Interior Department in 1939, and a year later merged into a single unit, the U.S. Fish and Wildlife Service.

The 1946 Fish and Wildlife Coordination Act officially committed the government to the policy that all new federal water projects would, if possible, include provisions to prevent loss or damage to fish and wildlife.[16] The 1946 act was amended in 1958 to make clear that in developing the nation's water resources, federal agencies were to treat fish and wildlife conservation as being of equal importance to the other purposes of federal water projects. While the act constituted a strong government commitment to wildlife conservation, provisions for enforcement were not included.

The first law passed by Congress specifically aimed at preservation of endangered species was the Endangered Species Act of 1966. That law instructed the Secretary of the Interior to take action to protect species of fish and wildlife in danger of extinction. Up to $15-million was authorized to acquire lands and waters to help preserve threatened species. In addition, the Secretary was authorized to use powers and funds available under other conservation laws to protect endangered wildlife.

In 1969 came the National Environmental Policy Act, which ordered every federal agency to determine the environmental impact of all actions that might significantly affect the quality of the environment. Those facts were to be used to determine whether proposed projects should proceed. The law was not aimed directly at wildlife preservation, but was indicative of the growing concern among Americans about the environment and ecology, including wildlife preservation and protection.

The Endangered Species Act of 1969 further amplified its 1966 predecessor. The new law widened the Interior Secretary's duties to insure that the United States did not contribute to the

---

[16] For details on wildlife legislation during the post-World War II period see Congressional Quarterly's *Congress and the Nation, 1945-1964*, pp. 1064-1068.

depredation of other nation's wildlife. A list of worldwide endangered species was drawn up and the law made it illegal to import any animal or product made from any animal on the list.

The Endangered Species Act of 1973

The Endangered Species Act of 1973, has been called "one of the most far-reaching animal protection bills ever enacted by any nation."[17] The law extended protection to fish and wildlife that were likely to become endangered, as well as those already officially listed as endangered by the Interior Department.[18]

Section VII of the 1973 Act has turned out to be the most important and most controversial part of the law. It directs the Secretary to insure that federal actions do not modify or destroy the "critical habitat" of any endangered species. Not only highly publicized endangered animals and birds, such as grizzly bears, alligators, bald eagles and whooping cranes, are included in this section, but also any living creatures which, in the words of the act, "are of esthetic, ecological, educational, historical, recreational, and scientific value to the nation and its people."

There was virtually no opposition to the act or to Section VII when it was passed by Congress in 1973. The agencies responsible for carrying out Section VII—the U.S. Fish and Wildlife Service and the National Marine Fisheries Service—published an interpretation of the term "critical habitat" on April 22, 1975. The next month, guidelines were developed to help other government agencies comply with the regulation.

Keith M. Schreiner, the Fish and Wildlife Service's associate director for federal assistance, who also is Endangered Species Program Manager, described how the government has interpreted Section VII: "Critical habitat is the area of land, water, and airspace required for the normal needs and survival of a species..." he wrote last year.[19] "The Service has defined these needs as space for growth, movement, and behavior; food and water sites for breeding and rearing of offspring; cover or shelter; and other biological or physical requirements."

Section VII has come under fire recently because of two widely publicized court suits brought by private groups trying to halt government projects that threatened the habitats of several endangered species. As a result of one of these suits, the U.S. Court of Appeals for the Sixth Circuit (Cincinnati), on Jan. 31,

---

[17] James D. Williams and Dona K. Finnley, "Our Vanishing Species: Can They Be Saved?" *Frontiers,* Summer 1977, p. 22.

[18] For a complete description of the law see Congressional Quarterly's *1973 Almanac,* pp. 670-672.

[19] In "Endangered Species Bulletin," published by the U.S. Fish and Wildlife Service, Endangered Species Program, August 1976, pp. 2, 4.

1977, ordered a halt to the Tennessee Valley Authority's Tellico Dam project, near Lenoir City, Tenn. The court held that continuing the dam would have violated the 1973 Endangered Species Act by destroying the habitat of a small minnow known as the snail darter.[20]

In the second case, the U.S. Supreme Court, on Nov. 30, 1976, upheld a lower court decision blocking construction of a six-mile, federally funded interstate highway interchange in Jackson County, Miss., near the habitat of the last 40 surviving Mississippi sandhill cranes. After the court's ruling, the highway was rerouted and some 26,000 acres of land were designated as the sandhill crane's critical habitat by the Interior Department.

These two court rulings raised the possibility that other federal projects could eventually be shelved. There has been a loud congressional reaction, especially from members whose districts are involved. Sens. James A. McClure (R Idaho) and Howard H. Baker Jr. (R Tenn.) called the Endangered Species Act inflexible. McClure and others have drawn up amendments to modify Section VII. Baker called for a review of the act by the Senate Environment and Public Works Committee. Subsequently the Subcommittee on Resource Protection completed three days of hearings on the matter in July. The panel heard from representatives of the American Mining Congress, the National Cattlemen's Association, the National Forest Products Association and others who testified that economic considerations should be paramount in evaluating the threat to endangered species and critical habitats from government building projects.

There was also testimony praising the act. Robert L. Herbst, an Assistant Secretary of the Interior, told the subcommittee that he strongly opposed any changes in the act. He pointed out that the Fish and Wildlife Service has handled more than 4,500 cases of potential endangered species conflicts in the last four years. Of those 4,500 cases, all but three were resolved administratively. The three that went to court were the Mississippi sandhill crane case, the snail darter case and a case involving the Indiana bat.[21] The Interior Department has drawn up a list of some 52 federal projects that could be halted because they may affect one or more threatened or endangered species. Based on the past record, most of those cases should be settled to the satisfaction of environmentalists, the government and others involved in the construction without legal action.

---

[20] The Tellico Dam project was begun in 1967.
[21] In this case, a U.S. District Court in Missouri ruled that the Meramec Park Dam near St. Louis could be built even though it would flood some caves inhabitated by the Indiana bat.

World Preservationist Movement

THE GROWING THREAT to wildlife is not just an American problem. Its scope is worldwide. The major cause of wildlife endangerment in the United States—mankind's encroachment into wilderness areas—is the same in the rest of the world, in both developed and developing countries. "Humanity is rapidly draining the earth of those materials which it requires for survival," Dr. Raymond F. Dasmann, senior ecologist for the International Union for the Conservation of Nature, told the International World Wildlife Conference last year.[22] Dasmann is among those who have warned repeatedly that civilization's march into former wilderness areas and the increasing consumption of the earth's raw materials are harming not only the world's wildlife, but all life on the planet.

The problem is often more acute in developing countries where few or no funds are available to spend on wildlife conservation programs. It has been estimated[23] that the world's tropical rain forests, which had been relatively untouched for 60 million years, currently are disappearing at the rate of 50 acres a minute.

Africa's Shrinking Elephant Population

The problem has been particularly evident in Africa, where the main concern of wildlife conservationists is the elephant. Elephants once roamed the entire African continent. Several centuries ago they vanished from North Africa. After the mid-17th century, the beasts began disappearing from most of southern Africa. Ian Douglas-Hamilton, a Scottish zoologist who headed an international study group investigating elephants in Tanzania, has estimated that there are at least one million elephants alive today in Africa. The study by Douglas-Hamilton, recognized as one of the world's leading elephant experts, showed that there has been a substantial decline in the number of elephants, even though figures on past populations are impossible to determine.

The Kenyan government took two steps last spring to aid its wildlife in general, and its elephants in particular. Big-game hunting was banned May 19 and a crackdown on poachers was announced May 31. "Anyone now found killing [any species of wildlife] is breaking the law," Kenya's Minister for Tourism and Wildlife, Matthew J. Ogutu, said recently.[24] Official figures

---

[22] Quoted in *The New York Times,* Dec. 1, 1976.
[23] By Sir Peter Scott of Great Britain, chairman of the World Wildlife Fund, in an address at the group's 1976 congress.
[24] Quoted in *The New York Times,* June 1, 1977.

131

released by the government of Kenya show that the elephant population of Tsavo National Park, located along the border with Tanzania, dropped from 35,900 in 1973 to 20,200 in 1975. The zebra population at a national park near Nairobi has fallen from 15,000 to 1,500 in two years. In Uganda, where it has been reported that the army has killed many elephants, the number has dropped to 2,200 today, from 14,000 in 1973, at the Kabalega Falls National Park.

Most of Africa's remaining elephants live in the center of the continent, where human habitation has least encroached on their hunting grounds. It is estimated that 80,000 to 110,000 are in Tanzania's Selous Game Reserve—a 21,000-square-mile preserve. While the threat from human encroachment is by far the most serious cause of the dwindling number of elephants, the demand for ivory—whose price has multiplied 10 times in the last five years—has led to a significant amount of illegal poaching of the beasts for their tusks.

Illegal Importation of Endangered Animals

A related worldwide concern is the smuggling of endangered species. A former animal hunter has estimated that 90 per cent of "all animals [that] dealers display have passed along...the chain of trafficking." That is, they have been involved in "trading of a more or less clandestine, shady and illicit nature."[25]

A section of the 1973 Endangered Species Act bans the importation into this country of any animal or product made from any animal listed on the worldwide endangered species list. The act amended and expanded sections dealing with importing endangered species found in the Lacey Act of 1900 and the 1966 Endangered Species Act *(see p. 128)*. During the first three years the 1973 law was in effect, agents of the U.S. Fish and Wildlife Service confiscated some $1-million worth of illegally imported goods—mostly hunting trophies, souvenirs and manufactured goods—at New York City's Kennedy International Airport alone. Included in the illegal goods were many items made from turtle shell, some 200 pairs of crocodile-skin shoes and fur clothing and pelts.

All confiscated items are stockpiled because they cannot be sold or auctioned, and the Fish and Wildlife Service currently has no authority to destroy them. Some of the goods are used by FWS personnel in programs to notify the public about the rules governing importation of endangered wildlife species. Exhibits have been set up at airports and in public schools explaining

---

[25] Jean-Yves Domalain, "Confessions of an Animal Trafficker," *Natural History,* May 1977, p. 54.

what types of goods are confiscated. There are dozens of FWS inspectors and agents who specialize in helping customs officials. Besides New York, the other FWS operations are located in the cities and ports through which wildlife products are required to be shipped: Miami, Chicago, San Francisco, Los Angeles, New Orleans, Seattle and Honolulu.

A parallel problem has been the organized wholesale importation of illegal wildlife products. In February 1973, a New York furrier and 32 other defendants were convicted of 50 counts of dealing in illegal animal pelts—mostly spotted cats from Brazil and Mexico. A government investigation showed that the company, Vesely-Forte, Inc., of New York, illegally imported some 101,000 pelts in 1971 and 1972. Included were pelts from ocelots, otters, leopards, cheetahs, jaguars, pumas and giant otters. Lewis Regenstein, executive vice president of The Fund for Animals, said the case proved the fur industry has "played a major role in causing the near-extinction of various forms of wildlife; and by continuing to create a demand for the skins of endangered species, they are providing an economic incentive for their illegal slaughter."[26]

International Efforts to Stop Smugglers

Beginning May 23, 1977, FWS regulations went into effect that have made the jobs of agents who oversee wildlife imports a little easier. The new rules were in conjunction with the 1973 Convention on International Trade in Endangered Species of Wild Fauna and Flora, a treaty that has been signed by some 80 nations, including the United States. The FWS-prepared regulations specify that permits or other documents are required for incoming international shipments of all wild plants and animals listed by the international convention as endangered or threatened. The convention's list does not totally concur with the official U.S. list of endangered species. FWS agents nevertheless anticipate a significant increase in the number of wildlife shipments refused entry because of improper identification. One reason is that such permits never have been required before and some importers are not aware of the new rules.

Another aspect of animal smuggling recently was brought to light when a federal grand jury in Philadelphia, on Aug. 4, indicted 12 persons on charges of illegally supplying endangered species of reptiles to eight American zoos. The indictments followed a two-and-a-half year investigation. The U.S. Attorney in Philadelphia characterized the traffic in illegal, rare and endangered species smuggled to zoos in this country as a "multimillion dollar business."[27] Most of the illegally shipped

[26] Quoted in *The Washington Post*, Feb. 22, 1973.
[27] Quoted in *The Washington Post*, Aug. 5, 1977.

Wildlife Support

Some of the major private organizations devoted to protecting endangered wildlife:

Defenders of Wildlife—Citizens' interest group that provides information about endangered species and wildlife in general.

National Audubon Society—Founded by George Bird Grinnell in 1901. Publishes bimonthly *Audubon* magazine. Promotes preservation of natural resources, including wildlife species. Headquarters in New York City. Edward H. Harte is chairman of the board.

National Wildlife Federation—Nonprofit, publicly supported conservation education organization. Promotes preservation of natural resources. Provides information on wildlife through a variety of publications.

Sierra Club—Citizens' interest group founded in 1892. Works in the United States and other countries to restore the quality of the natural environment and provides information on such subjects as wildlife, fish, forests, parks and recreation. Publishes monthly *Sierra Club Bulletin.* Headquarters in San Francisco, Calif.

The Fund for Animals—Citizens' interest group. Provides information about endangered species and other wildlife.

Wildlife Management Institute—Research and technical consulting organization funded by membership dues. Helps train wildlife specialists, provides scholarships and grants for advanced degree study, provides information about wildlife refuges and endangered species. Issues a biweekly newsletter, the "Outdoor News Bulletin."

World Wildlife Fund—Private, nonprofit publicly supported international conservation organization formed in 1961. Represented by 26 independent worldwide affiliates, including an American headquarters in Washington, D.C. Prince Bernhard of the Netherlands is international president. Supports scientific research and conservation projects to save endangered species and habitats. Sponsors a triennial international congress, the most recent of which was held in San Francisco in December 1976.

animals were snakes, lizards and crocodiles from Australia, Papua New Guinea, Fiji, Singapore, Ceylon and Madagascar.

Reptiles also are commonly shipped illicitly from Mexico and South America to dealers in the United States who sell them to private collectors. The FWS has estimated that the importing of such animals—usually poisonous snakes and beaded lizards—increased some 40 per cent last year from 1975. Another country from which a significant illicit exporting business originates is Australia. According to an Australian parliamentary committee which studied the problem last year, illegal wildlife smuggling from Australia is controlled for the most part by organized crime. Golden Shoulder parrots illegally shipped from Australia to the United States can sell for as much as $12,500 a pair.[28]

A lesser, but still persistent problem is the illegal hunting of endangered species in this country. FWS agents are stationed around the nation to investigate illegal hunting of such endangered species as Rocky Mountain goats and big horn sheep in California. While most game hunters obey the law, there have been instances of repeated willful violations. One such violation was discovered in January 1977 after a raid by 28 FWS agents on Tangier Island, Va., in the Chesapeake Bay. Undercover investigators had discovered that local guides were leading shooting expeditions for birds and fowl that were either out of season or on the endangered species list.

But pollution, population advances, and technological change pose the gravest threats to wildlife. As Michael Frome has written, "The alteration or destruction of habitat is more subtle than shooting, and equally deadly, though on a broader scale."[29] Frome and other environmentalists favor a large-scale method of conserving wildlife. Proposals to set up "ecosystems," total life communities functioning as ecological units in nature, have been suggested as the only way to stem the rising number of endangered species.

It is clear that the effort to conserve wildlife has advanced greatly in this country since the first wildlife preservation laws were passed more than a century ago. Many view the Endangered Species Act of 1973 as the most comprehensive and effective piece of American wildlife conservation legislation ever enacted. It has proven to be a versatile tool in the effort to help our wildlife survive today's pressures. But the list of endangered species continues to grow. And human population pressure and pollution continue to increase. Wildlife organizations, both public and private, have shifted their emphasis from the preservation of individual species to the preservation of natural habitats. But most agree that these measures will fall short until the highest form of animal stops polluting the earth and its air and water and stops squandering its natural resources. Ultimately, the fate of the world's wildlife is bound inextricably with man's.

---

[28] According to *The Christian Science Monitor*, Nov. 10, 1976.
[29] Frome, *op. cit.*, p. 76.

Selected Bibliography

Books

Carson, Rachel, *Silent Spring,* Fawcett, 1962.
Diole, Philippe, *The Errant Ark,* Putnam, 1974.
Domalain, Jean-Yves, *The Animal Connection,* William Morrow, 1977.
Frome, Michael, *Battle for the Wilderness,* Praeger, 1975.
Graham, Frank Jr., *Since Silent Spring,* Houghton Mifflin, 1970.
Leopold, Aldo, *A Sand County Almanac,* Oxford University Press, 1949.

Articles

Banker, Stephen, "And Now, Good News: Endangered Species is Saved," *Smithsonian,* January 1977.
Bean, Michael J., "The Endangered Species Act Under Fire," *National Parks & Conservation Magazine,* June 1977.
Davis, George M., "Rare and Endangered Species: A Dilemma," *Frontiers,* Summer 1977.
"Endangered Species: A Critical Crossroads," *The Environmental Journal,* February 1977.
Greenwalt, Lynn A., "A Place for Wildlife to Live," *American Forests,* December 1976.
Harcombe, P. A., and P. L. Marks, "Species Preservation," *Science,* Oct. 22, 1976.
Hopson, Janet L., "A Plea for a Mundane Mollusk," *The New York Times Magazine,* Nov. 14, 1976.
Laycock, George, "The Unhuntables are Finally Getting Attention, Funds," *Audubon,* May 1977.
——"Our Wildlife Refuges in Trouble," *Outdoor Life,* November 1976.
Nietschmann, Bernard, "The Nicaraguan Skin Connection," *Natural History,* January 1977.
Peterson, Russell W., "Wildlife and Man in the Street," *Vital Speeches of the Day,* Nov. 15, 1976.
Small, Frederick, "Eagles Nest—Classic Lesson in Wilderness Politics," *Audubon,* July 1977.
Storro-Patterson, Ronn, "Gray Whale Protection," *Oceans,* July 1977.
Wagner, James R., "Endangered Species Law Threatens Federal Project; Amendments Contemplated," *Congressional Quarterly,* March 12, 1977.

Reports and Studies

Bean, Michael J., "The Evolution of National Wildlife Law," Council on Environmental Quality, 1977.
Clark, William E., "Endangered Species of the United States," National Wildlife Federation, 1975.
Editorial Research Reports, "Wilderness Preservation," 1975 Vol. I, p. 382; "Wildlife Preservation," 1967 Vol. I, p. 341.
"Endangered Species Technical Bulletin," Department of the Interior, U.S. Fish and Wildlife Service, Endangered Species Program, selected issues.
"Outdoor News Bulletin," Wildlife Management Institute, selected issues.

Closing
THE
ENVIRONMENTAL
DECADE

by

William Sweet

Nov. 16
1 9 7 9

Editor's Note: The political reaction against environmentalism, which can be traced to mid-1979 when President Carter adopted a number of measures that antagonized members of conservation and ecology groups, took on an altogether new cast with the election of President Reagan. During the campaign, Reagan said he was opposed not to environmentalism as such, but only to environmental "extremism," which he considered responsible for problems in industries like steel. Soon after taking office, however, Reagan came to blows with environmentalists over the nomination of James G. Watt as secretary of the interior. A former head of the Mountain States Legal Foundation in Colorado, Watt had brought numerous suits against environmental regulations.

Despite strong opposition, Watt won confirmation and soon appointed like-minded individuals to key environmental positions throughout the government, notably, Robert Burford, former speaker of the Colorado legislature, as head of the Bureau of Land Management, and Ann McGill Gorsuch, a former member of the Colorado legislature, as administrator of the Environmental Protection Agency. Gorsuch has presided over sharp reductions in EPA's budget and personnel, and has tried to give states more responsibility for enforcing pollution control laws. Public support for environmental regulation has remained high, however, and environmental groups have exploited concern about Reagan's policies to recruit new members and raise money.

CLOSING THE ENVIRONMENTAL DECADE

NEW YEAR'S DAY 1980 will mark the tenth anniversary of the National Environmental Policy Act (NEPA), which had as its principal objective the encouragement of a "productive and enjoyable harmony between man and his environment." President Nixon made the NEPA signing ceremony on Jan. 1, 1970, his first official act of the new decade, saying that "the 1970s absolutely must be the years when America pays its debt to the past by reclaiming the purity of its air, its waters, and our living environment."[1] Many Americans agreed that the environment deserved far greater attention, and on April 22, 1970, less than four months after Nixon inaugurated the environmental decade, thousands of people gathered in cities and communities around the country to celebrate Earth Day.

Now that the Seventies are drawing to a close, many of the people who first met on Earth Day to demonstrate in favor of a better environment are planning to commemorate the occasion and celebrate the achievements of the past decade. But the festivities may be somewhat muted. For there is widespread fear that environmental concerns will fare poorly in the Eighties, as efforts to augment domestic energy supplies and reduce the costs associated with pollution abatement loom ever larger in the nation's affairs. President Carter, who received some of his strongest support from conservationists during his first two years in office, now is in trouble with environmentalists largely because of his attempts to expedite energy projects of urgent national interest.

To be sure, Americans are most unlikely to revert in the next decade to the habits of an era in which the quality of their air, water and land received little or no attention. In contrast to the situation 10 years ago, when environmentalists were widely regarded as kooky hippies who wanted to give up all the gifts of modern industrial civilization for the sake of returning to a mythical world of plants and animals, environmentalism today is firmly entrenched in the nation's consciousness. The jargon of environmentalism — "ecological balance," "recycling," "renewable resources" — has become a part of every educated person's working vocabulary. The small groups of activists who organized Earth Day in 1970 have developed into large, highly professional

---

[1] See "Environmental Policy," *E.R.R.*, 1974 Vol. II, pp. 945-964.

organizations. But such organizations probably will be working under increasingly adverse conditions in the Eighties, and most environmentalists doubt that the major legislative achievements of the 1970s will be duplicated in the next decade.

Major Legislation of the Past Ten Years

In the post-World War II period as a whole, only the civil rights legislation of the mid-1960s and the national security legislation of the late 1940s rival in importance the body of environmental legislation enacted during the Seventies. In addition to improving federal policy in certain traditional areas of environmental concern, such as land management and protection of endangered species *(see box)*, Congress authorized the establishment of new environmental procedures and agencies, passed laws to clean up the nation's air and water, and took steps to eliminate toxic chemicals from the environment. This corpus of legislation by itself would justify calling the Seventies the environmental decade.

The law which ushered in the decade, the National Environmental Policy Act, has been called an environmental "bill of rights" or "Magna Carta." Its most important provision required federal agencies to assess the effects of any "major federal action affecting the environment." In establishing the environmental impact statement, NEPA put a powerful tool into the hands of environmentalists. Individuals and groups now could challenge federal projects in the courts on the basis that the environmental impact had been inadequately assessed, and as it turned out the courts tended throughout the Seventies to enforce the law's requirements rigorously.

NEPA also established the Council on Environmental Quality to advise the president and to act as a kind of environmental ombudsman. Less than a year after the Council was set up, President Nixon recommended the establishment of the Environmental Protection Agency. EPA, which started operations on Dec. 2, 1970, took over responsibility for implementing environmental policies and for setting environmental standards for numerous federal agencies, including the National Air Pollution Control Administration, the Food and Drug Administration, and the Atomic Energy Commission. New legislation enacted in the following years greatly augmented EPA's responsibilities.

The Clean Air Act of 1970 set a schedule for reduction of automobile pollutants,[2] established federally enforced primary air-quality standards and state-enforced secondary standards, required states to prepare implementation plans for meeting secondary standards, and gave EPA the authority to rule on the

[2] See "Auto Emission Controls," *E.R.R.*, 1973 Vol. I, pp. 289-312.

Other Environmental Laws of the 1970s

Important environmental legislation enacted in the Seventies included, in addition to NEPA and pollution-control bills, the following laws:

Occupational Safety and Health Act of 1970. Authorized the secretary of labor, acting through the Occupational Safety and Health Administration, to set standards which employers must obey, including standards for toxics such as benzene, asbestos dust, vinyl chloride, cotton dust, and coke oven emissions.

Alaska Native Claims Settlement Act of 1971. Allowed the government to set aside 80 million acres of land in Alaska as national parks, forests and wildlife refuges.

Federal Environmental Pesticide Control Act of 1972. Required registration of all pesticides with the Environmental Protection Agency, which would be responsible for controlling their manufacture, distribution, and use.

Endangered Species Act of 1973. Prohibited federal projects that would destroy or modify a habitat crucial to the survival of an endangered species.

Safe Drinking Water Act of 1974. Directed the Environmental Protection Agency to set maximum levels for certain chemical and bacteriological pollutants.

Federal Land Policy and Management Act of 1976. Updated and consolidated about 3,000 public laws pertaining to management of federal lands by the Bureau of Land Management.

Federal Mine Safety and Health Act of 1977. Transferred regulatory authority over all types of mines from the Department of Interior to the Department of Labor, applied a single statute to both coal and non-coal mines, expedited procedures for setting standards, imposing penalties and collecting fines, and included a toxics provision to assure "the highest degree of health and safety protection."

Surface Mining Control and Reclamation Act of 1977. Set performance standards to be met by all major coal strip-mining operations and protected certain lands as unsuitable for surface mining.

adequacy of state plans. Congress revised standards and extended deadlines several times after 1970, notably in the Energy Supply and Environmental Coordination Act of 1974 and the Clean Air Amendments of 1977, but the basic policy of reducing automobile pollutants has remained intact and states currently are required to meet standards for pollutants from stationary sources by Dec. 31, 1982. The Clean Air Amendments of 1977 set guidelines for "non-deterioration" of areas already in compliance with standards, and the 1974 Energy Supply Act extended deadlines for fuel-burning plants to provide for increased use of coal rather than oil.

At least as important as the clean air laws was the legislation to clean the nation's waters. The Water Quality Improvement Act of 1970 made petroleum companies liable for up to $14 million in oil-spill clean-up costs, strengthened restrictions on thermal pollution from nuclear power plants, ordered EPA to develop criteria covering the effects of pesticides in streams, rivers and other waters, and created an Office of Environmental Quality to act as staff for the Council on Environmental Quality. Still more comprehensive were the Water Pollution and Control Act Amendments of 1972, which set a national goal of eliminating all pollutant discharges into U.S. waters by 1985.[3]

The amendments required industries to use the "best practicable control technology currently available" by July 1, 1977, and the "best available technology economically achievable" by July 1, 1983. The amendments also authorized $24.6 billion to be spent on cleaning the nation's waters, including $18 billion in federal construction grants to states for building waste treatment plants.

The Resource Recovery Act of 1970 already had set up a modest program of demonstration and construction grants for innovative solid waste management systems.[4] In 1976, Congress passed the Resource Conservation and Recovery Act and the Toxic Substances Control Act, which gave EPA wide powers to set restrictions on disposal of toxic wastes and other hazardous substances. The Resource Conservation and Recovery Act set "cradle-to-grave" standards covering the generation and disposal of wastes, and the Toxic Substances Control Act required EPA to prepare guidelines for handling all toxic substances, with the exception of drugs, cosmetics and tobacco.[5]

Toting Up the Balance Sheet for a Decade

The National Wildlife Federation asserted in its tenth annual Environmental Quality Index, which it published early in 1979, that an "Environmental Revolution" comparable to the Industrial Revolution had taken place.[6] Not only did the decade produce "most of the basic legislation needed for environmental reform," but the public got "into decision-making at all levels of government" and "year after year, national opinion surveys constantly reveal[ed] a solid mass of public support for improved environmental quality." Because of that support, environmental arguments repeatedly "saved the day when the main issue seemed to be something else." The supersonic transport project, though economically dubious, was dropped mainly because of objections connected with noise, stratospheric pollu-

---

[3] See "Pollution Control: Costs and Benefits," *E.R.R.*, 1976 Vol. I, pp. 145-164.
[4] See "Solid Waste Technology," *E.R.R.*, 1974 Vol. II, pp. 641-664.
[5] See "Toxic Substance Control," *E.R.R.*, 1978 Vol. II, pp. 741-760.
[6] Gladwin Hill, "1969-1979: A Decade of Revolution," *National Wildlife*, February-March 1979, pp. 17-32.

tion, and fuel inefficiency; the Alaska pipeline project was drastically modified to meet environmental concerns; and the nation's nuclear power plant construction was sharply curtailed.[7]

Surveying the overall effects of environmentalist reform, however, the Wildlife Federation was rather more guarded in its enthusiasm. While a nationwide network of air-quality monitoring stations has been set up and even though 90 percent of the major U.S. factories are in compliance with pollution laws, the federation noted that most Americans continue to live in areas where the air is unsafe to breathe. "...[O]f the nation's 105 largest urban areas, only Honolulu has really clean air," and "smog remains a serious problem in nearly a fourth of the country's 3,200 counties."

NATIONAL ENVIRONMENTAL POLICY ACT OF 1969
P.I. 91-190, see page 950

Senate Report (Interior and Insular Affairs Committee) No. 91-296, July 9, 1969 [To accompany S. 1075]

House September 23, December 22, 1969
No. 91-378, July 11, 19, 1969 [To accompany H.R. 12549]

Conference Report No. 91-765, Dec. 17, 1969
[To accompany S. 1075]

Cong. Record Vol. 115 (1969)

DATES OF CONSIDERATION AND PASSAGE

Senate July 10, December 20, 1969

House September 23, December 22, 1969

The Senate bill was passed in lieu of the House bill after substituting for its language much of the text of the House bill. The House Report and the Conference Report are set out.

HOUSE REPORT NO. 91-378

THE Committee on Merchant Marine and Fisheries, to whom was referred the bill (H.R. 12549), to amend the Fish and Wildlife Coordination Act to provide for the establishment of a Council on Environmental Quality, and for other purposes, having considered the same, report favorably thereon with an amendment and recommend that the bill as amended do pass.

PURPOSE OF THE BILL

The purpose of the bill, as hereby reported, is to create a Council on Environmental Quality with a broad and independent overview of current and long-term trends in the quality of our national environment, to ad-

Some 50 bodies of water, according to the Wildlife Federation, "have shown considerable improvement," and "about 3,600 of the nation's 4,000 major industrial polluters are meeting their clean-up deadlines." But the federation said scientists have been discovering new sources of water pollution faster than the known sources have been eliminated. In the matter of toxics, especially, the government has only just begun to assess the 10,000 landfill sites around the country "that have been used to get rid of up to 45 million tons of chemical wastes annually."

Because so many problems remain to be solved, environmentalists dearly hope to make as much progress in the Eighties as they did in the Seventies. A new consortium of national conservation groups, the Coast Alliance, plans to make 1980 the "Year of the Coasts." The alliance will encourage local groups to sponsor a variety of events and at the same time push for revision of federal laws affecting America's coastlines.[8]

Another group, the Citizens Committee for a Second Environmental Decade, plans to stage "Earth Day 80" on the tenth

[7] Congress in 1971 terminated federal support for the development of a commercial supersonic passenger transport (SST) plane, to compete with the British-French Concorde. For background, see Congressional Quarterly's *Congress and the Nation*, Vol. III, pp. 167-168. The Trans-Alaska Pipeline Authorization Act of 1973 overrode environmental objections to the construction of a pipeline from the North Slope to the ice-free port of Valdez, but by the time the came into operation in 1977 the project had been substantially modified to meet environmental concerns.

[8] See "Making Waves," *Environmental Action*, September 1979, p. 4. See also "Coastal Zone Management," *E.R.R.*, 1976 Vol. II, pp. 863-882.

anniversary of the 1970 Earth Day to mobilize support for a renewed effort at improving the nation's quality of life. The Citizens Committee is a coalition of environmentalist leaders, national organizations and local groups. The emphasis is on local activitiy. Michael McCabe, executive director of Earth Day 80, said, "the most important legislation is complete at the national level, and the main task now will be implementation of laws and development of new issues."[9]

As former staff director of the Congressional Environmental Study Conference, an office which provides members of Congress with a weekly bulletin and background papers on legislative issues pertaining to the environment, McCabe does not completely discount prospects for continued legislative progress. From the time the study conference was founded in 1975, its membership has grown to include 72 senators and 245 representatives to become "the largest ad hoc organization in Congress."

Conflict With Energy Priority and Carter

According to estimates prepared by the Council on Environmental Quality, the nation as a whole — including both government and private industry — spent about $47.6 billion for pollution control in 1978.[10] Of that amount, less than half resulted from environmental legislation; but the CEQ estimates did not take into account the clean air and water pollution amendments of 1977 and the Resource Conservation and Toxic Substances Control Acts of 1976. When their costs are figured in, pollution abatement costs attributed to federal regulations go higher. The council projects the total costs resulting from federal laws at $361.3 billion for the years 1977 through 1986.

While the benefits of environmental regulation cannot easily be measured in dollars, almost everybody agrees that the costs will be increasingly hard to bear in a period of oil shortages, rampant inflation and economic recession. Because of such economic constraints, the political environment already is becoming more inhospitable to environmentalism, and one result has been a drastic change in President Carter's standing among environmentalists.

Carter appealed strongly to the environmentalists during his 1976 campaign, and during his first two years in office received high marks from them. At a press conference held in Washington on Dec. 20, 1978, over 30 environmentalist leaders gave Carter an "outstanding" rating for his performance, noting especially his efforts to protect Alaska wilderness, the high quality of

[9] Interview, Oct. 30, 1979. *Environmental Action,* which was founded by organizers of the first Earth Day, plans to support Earth Day 80 by encouraging the some 6,000 local groups with which it maintains contacts to stage events.

[10] Council on Environmental Quality, *Annual Report: 1978,* pp. 424, 428.

his appointments to environmental positions, and his attempts to block water projects they considered wasteful.[11] Environmentalists already had begun to worry, though, about remarks some administration officials were making about the necessity of assessing the inflationary impact of environmental regulation.

By the summer of 1979 the honeymoon was over. Carter sorely strained his relations with environmentalists on two occasions. First, on July 15 in a televised speech to the nation about energy needs, he said: "We will protect the environment. But if the nation needs to build a pipeline or a refinery — we will build them." In the days following the speech, Carter spelled out plans for an $88-billion synthetic fuels program and the creation of an Energy Mobilization Board with authority to bypass environmental standards.[12] Second, on Sept. 25 Carter signed into law a bill directing completion of the Tellico Dam in Tennessee.

The controversy over Tellico turned on the danger it posed to an endangered species, the tiny snail darter, which came to symbolize for environmentalists the broader threat that Congress would increasingly waive existing legislation for the sake of expediting priority projects. When Carter signed the bill exempting Tellico from all existing restrictions in federal law, the League of Conservation Voters sharply criticized his leadership, saying he lacked the nerve to stand up to Congress. Brock Evans, director of the Sierra Club's Washington office, said the president had "sent a clear message to anybody who worries about laws that stand in the way of pork barrel projects — 'don't worry about my views, I won't veto them.' "[13]

In decrying Carter's apostasy, environmentalists cite public opinion polls which continue to indicate — despite the country's economic problems — support for higher spending on pollution abatement.[14] *Audubon* magazine noted more sympathetically that Tellico was a hard decision for Carter to make. "His heart said veto. But practical politics said yes."[15] Many environmentalists recognize that the tide may be turning against them and that the environmental decade may be, in hindsight, just that — *the* environmental decade.

---

[11] In 1977 Carter tried to stop the federal financing of 19 water projects (dams, canals, etc.) as environmentally unsound and economically wasteful. Conservationists were delighted, but his plan met with stiff opposition in Congress and had to be substantially modified.

[12] See "Synthetic Fuels," *E.R.R.*, 1979 Vol. II, pp. 621-640. On Oct. 4. the Senate agreed to create an Energy Mobilization Board that could waive certain procedural requirements in order to expedite priority energy projects. On Nov. 1, the House agreed to a separate bill that would let the board waive certain substantive laws as well, with the permission of the president and both houses of Congress. The two versions of the Mobilization Board legislation now go to House-Senate conference to work out differences.

[13] Quoted in *The Washington Star*, Sept. 27, 1979.

[14] See for example Robert Cameron Mitchell, "Silent Spring — Solid Majorities," *Public Opinion*, August-September 1979, pp. 16-20.

[15] Robert Cahn, "Perspective: The Triumph of Wrong," *Audubon*, November 1979, p. 12.

Origins of Environmentalism

ENVIRONMENTALISM has roots going back more than a century, but the modern environmental movement as we know it today is of recent vintage, so recent that dictionaries have failed to keep pace with the concept. The 1977 edition of Webster's *New Collegiate Dictionary* defines environmentalism as "a theory that views environment rather than heredity as the important factor in the development and especially the cultural and intellectual development of an individual." This definition altogether misses the concern for the protection of nature that is at the heart of modern environmentalism, and it contains a view of heredity that few people would defend today.

Webster's definition seems to refer to the views espoused by some enlightenment philosophers in the 18th century, who thought that the environment completely determined human nature, and who believed that by perfecting the environment one could also perfect mankind. But modern environmentalists fear that it is precisely man's efforts to manipulate the environment which may be undermining the natural relationships that sustain all life on earth. In sharp contrast to the 18th century philosophers, modern environmentalists view life as a delicate balance of genetic and environmental factors, which is understood only partially and manipulated at mankind's peril.

Modern environmentalism, in fact, is rooted not so much in the 18th century as in the 19th century. Two developments account for its emergence. One was the publication in 1859 of Charles Darwin's *Origin of the Species,* which inspired systematic scientific research into the question of how groups of organisms adapt to their habitats. The other was the industrial revolution. By the end of the 1800s, squalid manufacturing cities, belching locomotives, and abysmal mining centers blighted the landscape and, often, the lives of the people.

Darwin advanced the theory in the *Origin of the Species* that evolution results from a process he called natural selection, or "survival of the fittest." Changes in individual organisms occur spontaneously as the result of hereditary factors, he said, and those organisms with the characteristics most suitable for their habitats survive. In Darwin's theory, which virtually all scientists now accept, evolution is equally the product of hereditary and environmental factors.

Publication of the *Origin of the Species* soon led to the creation of a new scientific field called "ecology." In 1869, the German biologist Ernst Haeckel stated that the individual was a product of cooperation between the environment and organismal heredity. He termed this relationship "oecology," a word derived from the Greek meaning "house," and indicating the study of organisms in their natural environments. In the 1890s, ecology "was placed on a modern basis, more or less," by scientists working in Switzerland, Denmark and the United States. "Thereafter, research in ecological subjects tended to stress population and community analysis."[16]

Coincidentally, it was also in the 1890s that the first conservationist and naturalist social movements appeared. By then the industrial revolution was firmly entrenched in England, and the new industrial city of Manchester had become the world's leading symbol of all that industrialization meant — both good and bad. On the one hand, the Manchester School of political and economic liberalism, led by Richard Cobden and John Bright, maintained that absolutely free trade and unrestricted competition would lead to universal prosperity and world peace. On the other hand, critics of the industrial revolution from the political far left to the far right held that Manchester epitomized all that was dehumanizing about industrialization.

In Germany, where social critics were able to observe economic and political developments in England and France before they took hold in the "Fatherland," Manchester became a particularly potent symbol of what the future held in store. On the left, Karl Marx, working in collaboration with Friedrich Engels, the heir to a Manchester textile firm founded by his father, made Manchester a case study in his critique of industrial capitalism. On the right, numerous writers frequently invoked Manchester's squalor as an example of what "decadent bourgeois liberalism" would inevitably lead to.

It was in Germany where a sort of "back to the land" youth movement first developed, and around the turn of the century it became a firmly established social custom for adolescents to spend a year or two wandering about in natural surroundings before settling down.[17] Vulgarized Darwinian ideas connected with a cult of physical strength and racial purity had some play in the German youth movement, and they became an important ideological element in Hitler's imperialistic policies in Eastern Europe: his "push to the East" in search of *Lebensraum* — living space — for the German people.

Reformist Roots of American Environmentalism

In the United States industrialization proceeded in the late 19th century closely in tandem with Germany's economic development, and here too the first conservationist social movements

---

[16] Thomas Park, "Ecology," *Encyclopaedia Britannica* (1973), Vol. 7, p. 913. Park is a former president of the American Association for the Advancement of Science.

[17] See Walter Z. Laqueur, *Young Germany* (1962), p. 15.

emerged in the 1890s in response to fears that industrial squalor soon would destroy all remaining wilderness. But in the United States conservationism took hold with an especially strong grip, apparently because the first boom period of industrial capitalism coincided with the closing of the frontier. In 1890, as Frederick Jackson Turner pointed out on the first page of his famous essay on "The Significance of the Frontier in American History," the superintendent of the census announced that "there can hardly be said to be a frontier line" and that the frontier therefore could no longer "have a place in the census reports."[18] The closing of the frontier meant, among other things, that industry now would expand in a confined space and that individuals no longer would be able to escape industrialization simply by moving West.

On June 4, 1892, a group of people inspired by the naturalist-writer John Muir drew up the articles of incorporation for the Sierra Club. Many of these people were San Francisco professionals, and what they had in common was a love for the Yosemite Valley, which they wanted to protect from commercial exploitation. Meanwhile, on the other side of the continent, the first Audubon societies were founded in Massachusetts and Pennsylvania. Their main objective was to save bird and mammal species from extinction at the hands of plume hunters for the millinery trade and other commercial interests. Between 1895 and 1905 the first Audubon groups persuaded 32 states to enact bird protection laws, and in 1905 the groups incorporated in New York City as a national association.

The emergence of industrial capitalism and the closing of the frontier bred, in addition to conservationist movements, mounting concern about the deteriorating urban environment and the increasing monopolization of public resources. Muckrakers such as Lincoln Steffens (*The Shame of the Cities*, 1904), Ida Tarbell (*History of Standard Oil*, 1904), and Upton Sinclair (*The Jungle*, 1906), drew attention to the perils associated with unbridled industrial growth, not only in their books but also in a series of influential magazines such as *McClure's* and *Collier's*.

These reformers, Turner said, were "sounding the warning that American democratic ideals and society are menaced . . . by the very conditions that make this apparent prosperity; that the economic resources are no longer limitless and free; that the aggregate national wealth is increasing at the cost of present social justice and moral health, and the future well-being of the American people. The Granger and the Populist were prophets of this reform movement. Mr. [William Jennings] Bryan's

---

[18] Quoted by Frederick Jackson Turner in his book *The Frontier in American History* (1921), p. 1.

Democracy, Mr. [Eugene Victor] Debs' Socialism, and Mr. [Theodore] Roosevelt's Republicanism all had in common the emphasis upon the need of governmental regulation of industrial tendencies in the interest of the common man...."[19]

As president from 1901 to 1909, Theodore Roosevelt conducted constant battles with the great trusts and combinations, and he saved extensive areas of the public domain from exploitation by private interests. He also was the first president to call attention to the problem of resource scarcity: In 1907 he summoned the governors of 46 states to ponder the danger of exhausting the nation's natural resources. But Roosevelt had an ambivalent relationship with the reformers, whom he was the first to call "muckrakers," referring to the Muck-raker in John Bunyan's *Pilgrim's Progress* who was so concerned with raking filth that he could not see the celestial crown offered him. And like other environmentalists after him, Roosevelt also was ambivalent about the closing of the frontier.[20]

New Knowledge About the Biological Chain

By World War I all major components of modern environmentalism had emerged: the science of ecology; conservationist and naturalist social movements; the critique of the urban and industrial environment created by unbridled industrial competition; and the concern about private exploitation of dwindling public resources. Why then did it take over 50 years for these strands to coalesce into a major national movement?

Part of the explanation would seem to be connected with a flood of external events that interrupted the development of environmentalism and had an especially disruptive effect on those who sought greater social control over the disposition of public resources. World War I, then the government raids against the political left in 1919, the unfettered capitalism of the 1920s, the Great Depression of the 1930s, World War II and finally the Cold War, each in turn created an inhospitable political atmosphere for doctrines of limited economic growth.

At the same time, some aspects of environmentalism, while very much alive, had yet to mature. The Sierra Club ceased to be merely a California organization and to acquire a national membership only in the 1940s. The Izaak Walton League and Wilderness Society were founded only in 1922 and 1935, respectively. The science of ecology, similarly, had a long way to go from being a mere concept to becoming a full-fledged research activity pursued by thousands of experts.

---

[19] *Ibid.*, p. 281.

[20] John F. Kennedy, similarly, was sympathetic to environmental concerns and campaigned with the slogan "The New Frontier" in 1960. Today, Gov. Edmund G. (Jerry) Brown Jr. of California espouses environmental concerns vigorously but also speaks frequently of outer space as America's new frontier.

Particularly important to the history of ecology were advances in population genetics, which researchers working in the United States, England and the Soviet Union developed into a precise mathematical science during the 1910s and 1920s. By the 1930s and 1940s, according to science historian Garland Allen, there was an "increasing realization that all biological phenomena are interconnected and could be dealt with in similar terms." Those terms were largely derived from genetics, Allen said, but they were applied in a new context, namely, "of the organism or population as an entity, a reacting system meaningful only in the context of its environmental surroundings."[21]

The advances in population genetics, and the development of increasingly refined techniques for tracing chemical substances through the biological chain, helped stimulate more and more detailed research into the interaction of individual species with their habitats. This was true not only within America's growing university complex, but also among amateur naturalists, and within newly organized government agencies such as the Fish and Wildlife Service, which was established in 1940. The person who by all accounts did more than any other individual to stimulate the creation of the contemporary environmental movement, Rachel Carson, was intimately familiar with all these aspects of ecological research.

Rachel Carson's Profound Public Influence

Carson did graduate work in genetics at Johns Hopkins University and post-graduate work at the Marine Biological Laboratory in Woods Hole, Mass. She had a profound love of nature and also happened to be a writer of considerable ability. In 1936 she went to work for the U.S. Bureau of Fisheries, which later became part of the Fish and Wildlife Service, and she subsequently became writer, then editor, and finally editor-in-chief of the Wildlife Service's publications.

In 1951 Carson published *The Sea Around Us,* a book about marine ecology which not only met with high acclaim among professional scientists but also stayed on the best-seller lists for 86 weeks. During the late 1950s she became deeply concerned about the effects such persistent pesticides as DDT were having on the natural environment, and during the final years of her life, while she was dying of cancer, she devoted herself to studying the pesticide problem. That work led to the publication of *Silent Spring,* first in an abridged version in *The New Yorker* in June 1961, then as a book in 1962. The title reflects her portrayal of an environment so poisoned that eventually it would be left without the birds and insects that provide the sounds of spring.

The publication of *Silent Spring* provoked fierce attacks from

[21] Garland Allen, *Life Science in the Twentieth Century* (1975), p. 144.

interests that had a hand in the pesticide business. Velsicol Chemical Corp. tried to get Houghton Mifflin to drop publication, objecting that the book created the "false impression that all business is grasping and immoral" and that it would lead to reduced use of "agricultural chemicals in this country and in the countries of western Europe, so that our supply of food will be reduced to east-curtain parity [Soviet-bloc levels]."[22] When CBS did a television program on April 3, 1963, called "The Silent Spring of Rachel Carson," three of the program's five sponsors withdrew just days before it was to be broadcast.[23]

Despite such pressures, Carson's work came to the attention of President Kennedy, who happened to be a reader of *The New Yorker.* On May 15, 1963, his Science Advisory Committee's pesticide panel issued a report calling for "orderly reduction in the use of pesticides." Beginning nine years later with a ban on most DDT uses, several pesticides have been restricted.

While Carson was instrumental in demonstrating what decades of neglect and abuse had done to America's ecology, and while she showed that powerful vested interests could be defeated, most observers of environmentalism

Rachel Carson

attribute the movement's coalescence in the late 1960s to a variety of other factors as well. In 1966, the first photos from outer space showed the entire globe and brought home to millions, as nothing ever had before, that human beings are one race confined to one geographic space. Then there were offshore oil spills that drew public attention.

Finally, a number of important changes were drastically altering the nation's social and political atmosphere. The civil rights and anti-war movements, together with the coming of age of the baby-boom generation, led to widespread questioning of authority of all kinds. At the same time, disillusionment with suburbia was beginning to manifest itself. Many people had fled the cities in the hope of living close to nature, and what many of them found instead were endless strings of superhighways, fast food chains and used car lots.[24]

---

[22] Quoted by Frank Graham Jr. in *Since Silent Spring* (1970), p. 49.

[23] They were Standard Brands and Ralston Purina, both major agribusiness concerns, and Lehn and Fink Products, manufacturer of Lysol.

[24] Gus Speth, chairman of the CEQ, stressed the importance of this last point in an interview, Oct. 29, 1979.

Changes in the Movement

THE COMBINATION of influences that came into play in the 1960s soon led to the foundation of numerous new environmental groups, many of which had objectives going far beyond traditional conservationist concerns. The controversy over persistent pesticides, for example, led to the creation of one of that decade's most influential organizations. In 1966 a New York lawyer, Victor Yannocone, brought suit against the Suffolk County (Long Island) Mosquito Control Commission on behalf of his wife, who was worried about the effects of local DDT spraying. Yannocone lost the suit, despite financial assistance from Audubon and technical advice from scientists at the Brookhaven National Laboratory and the State University of New York at Stony Brook, but the case inspired him to found the Environmental Defense Fund (EDF). As an organization combining scientists and lawyers, EDF went on to bring many successful suits on behalf of environmental interests.[25]

A similar organization, the Natural Resources Defense Council, was founded in 1970 by a group of students at Yale Law School. Inspired by the National Association for the Advancement of Colored People's Legal Defense Fund, the students wanted to advance environmental interests in the courts. The Ford Foundation became interested in the project and put the students in touch with a New York group, the Scenic Hudson Preservation Conference, which was fighting to block a hydroelectric project at Storm King Mountain along the Hudson River. Together the two groups formed the NRDC, and like the Environmental Defense Fund, NRDC brought many important and successful law suits in the Seventies.

A more purely scientific environmental organization, the Union of Concerned Scientists (UCS), was organized in 1969 by student activists at the Massachusetts Institute of Technology who wanted to take public positions on the misuse of technology — primarily in Vietnam and in the strategic arms race. Much of UCS's work soon came to be focused on the issue of nuclear safety, and some persons whom the organization backed — notably Dan Ford and Henry Kendall — became the nation's leading critics of the emergency core cooling system designed for nuclear power plants.

While groups like EDF, UCS and NRDC have their strongest roots in the scientific community, other groups founded in the Seventies hearken back to the Progressive and socialist traditions of muckrakers Ida Tarbell, Lincoln Steffens and Upton

---

[25] See Joel Primack and Frank von Hippel's *Advice and Dissent: Scientists in the Political Arena* (1974), pp. 128-142.

Sinclair. Environmental Action is a group best known for its "Dirty Dozen" campaign every two years to defeat 12 members of Congress selected for their anti-environment voting record. This organization emphasizes the urban environment along with more conventional ecological concerns such as bottle recycling and toxics. The Environmentalists for Full Employment, founded in 1976 with the support of about 100 sponsoring groups, works with labor, urban and environmental groups on issues of mutual concern. The Urban Environmental Conference, founded in 1971, is a coalition of organizations ranging from the National Urban League to the United Steel Workers.

As groups based in scientific and progressive political traditions have carved out a sizable role for themselves, the older conservationist organizations have responded to the challenge by broadening their concerns and by adopting the most modern political tactics. The Alaska Coalition, which has been urging the government since early in 1977 to set aside 170 million acres of Alaska as parks and refuges, represents the most impressive single effort that has been organized by conservationists. The coalition has employed computerized lists, phone banks, some 10,000 volunteers, and three separate professional staffs to work on grass-roots organizing, lobbying, and media relations.[26]

Criticism That Elitism, Anti-Science Prevail

Critics of environmentalism have accused the movement of promoting an irrational suspicion of science and technology, and of furthering the interests of a privileged few at the expense of the vast majority of ordinary Americans. "The talk of survival, limited resources and austerity does not crimp the lifestyle of suburban environmentalists, but only of the people they keep outside," asserts Bernard Frieden, a professor at the Massachusetts Institute of Technology.[27]

From its earliest days environmentalism has been vulnerable to pseudo-scientific ideas, and many of the early conservationists really were members of a social elite that could afford to enjoy the splendors of undisturbed nature. Most of the people who staff the leading environmental groups today are products of the nation's social and educational elite, and many of the people they claim to represent do indeed express an indiscriminate hostility to all things modern.

Even so, the critics of environmentalism may be somewhat undiscriminating, unable to discern its numerous strains — some scientific and some anti-scientific, some left-wing in their political orientation and some right-wing. Competition among

[26] See Gail Robinson's "The Lessons of the Alaska Coalition," *Environmental Action*, Sept. 23, 1978, pp. 10-11.

[27] Bernard Frieden, author of *The Environmental Protection Hustle* (1979), quoted in "Environmentalism: Assessing the Impact," *Energy Daily*, Aug. 2, 1979, p. 4.

the different approaches to environmentalism tends to keep the movement alert and self-critical, and as the Seventies have drawn to a close, fresh ideas and strong personalities have continued to breed new organizations representing varied constituencies.

One trend which many observers expect to become stronger in the Eighties is a preoccupation with technical issues. Whereas passage of legislation tended to be the goal in the Seventies, the emphasis in the Eighties is likely to be on carrying out existing laws. Local groups have a greater voice in how national objectives are met in specific situations, such as in state implementation plans required by clean air legislation. And several national organizations devote considerable attention to monitoring the activities of government agencies in a broad array of environmental fields. The Environmental Policy Center, for example, does highly regarded technical work on a wide range of issues.

EPC was founded in 1972 by people who had broken away from the Friends of the Earth, which itself was established in 1969 by David Brower shortly after he left the Sierra Club as executive director. FOE concentrates on global issues such as nuclear proliferation and world energy policy, typifying a trend in environmentalism at an opposite extreme from the technical and local issues which other groups prefer to work on. Many environmental problems — such as rising carbon dioxide levels, acid rain and global population growth — transcend national boundaries and can be solved only by means of cooperation among environmentalists working in many countries.

Friends of the Earth has branches in 22 countries, and some such as the British and French branches are highly influential. Other organizations such as Worldwatch in Washington, D.C., and The Institute for World Order in New York City specialize in a more scholarly approach to global issues, after the fashion of the peace research institutes which were set up decades ago in countries such as Sweden, Norway and Holland.[28]

Urban Environment and Financing in the 1980s

Another area likely to receive more attention is the urban environment. Most Americans, after all, live in urban areas. Rep. Joseph L. Fisher, D-Va., former president of Resources for the Future and the current co-chairman of the Environmental Study Conference, thinks that legislative efforts now "must go beyond pollution, toxics, and so forth, and take on the broader dimensions of the urban environment such as congestion." Fisher, who has served extensively on local planning boards in

---

[28] The best known of these is the Stockholm International Peace Research Institute, a leading independent authority on global military trends.

Virginia, believes that the broad problems can be solved only by means of long-range planning and that the federal government can do much to assist localities in improving their planning capabilities.[29]

Fisher, as a political moderate who approaches problems in a pragmatic fashion, hopes to prevent the 1980s from becoming a "period of confrontation between energy proponents and environmentalists." Many environmentalists are far less sanguine than Fisher about the effects of energy shortages and economic stagnation in the 1980s. To be sure, environmental regulation may have less harmful effects on employment than is generally imagined. Data Resources Inc., in a study completed in January 1979, estimated that in the period 1970-1986 the unemployment rate would be lower with pollution control expenditures than without.[30]

One direct effect of inflation and fears of a recession, however, is that contributions to environmental groups have slowed at a time their programs are expanding. In the case of the organizations that specialize in legal work, such as EDF and NRDC, a withdrawal of Ford Foundation money has compounded difficulties. While Ford had been expected to cut funding eventually, since the foundation has a policy of not financing projects in perpetuity, the cuts come at a time when it is exceptionally difficult to raise money from other sources.

But while some individual groups may go under in the 1980s, there is little doubt that environmentalism as a movement will survive a period of austerity. Gus Speth, chairman of the Council on Environmental Quality, comments: "People still have to care about the environment because it affects them in so many ways: oil spills, emphysema, cancer, recreation, food, resource questions. These problems are going to stay until they're solved."[31]

A major problem facing environmentalism in the 1980s is likely to be harmonization of internal differences, as the movement embraces more and more wide-ranging concerns. Environmentalists already are quite bitterly divided on some of the major policy issues of the day. Conservationist organizations tended to favor Carter's plan for oil-price decontrol, while groups aligned with urban, minority, and labor interests preferred rationing and stricter public regulation of the energy corporations. In the sensitive area of population policy, environmentalists are divided between those who would minimize

---

[29] Interview, Nov. 1, 1979.

[30] Study cited by Charles Doherty in "The Economic Impact of a Clean Environment," *The AFL-CIO American Federationist*, October 1979, pp. 3-4.

[31] Interview, Oct. 29, 1979.

any additional immigration into the United States and those who believe that this country should do more to relieve poor countries of their population pressures. A recent article in *Environmental Action* magazine advocating open immigration into the United States from Mexico touched off a storm of indignation among environmentalists.[32]

Environmentalists — like many of the species they try to protect — have displayed a formidable capacity for spontaneous change and growth in unexpected directions. But unlike many of the organisms that geneticists like to study in their natural habitats, environmentalists live in a global habitat which itself is changing rapidly in unpredictable directions. Any number of strains in environmentalism could prove suitable to the needs of the 1980s, and depending on how successful those strains are in competition with other emerging social trends, the Eighties may or may not be yet another environmental decade.

[32] See Rice Odell's "The Illegal Immigration Bugaboo," *Environmental Action,* June 1979, pp. 14-15, and November 1979, pp. 2-3, for responses.

Selected Bibliography

Books

Allen, Garland, *Life Science in the Twentieth Century,* John Wiley and Sons, 1975.

Carson, Rachel, *Silent Spring,* Houghton Mifflin Co., 1962.

Gilliam, Ann, ed., *Voices for the Earth: A Treasury of the Sierra Club Bulletin: 1893-1977,* Sierra Club Books, 1979.

Graham, Frank Jr., *Since Silent Spring,* Houghton Mifflin Co., 1970.

Nash, Roderick, ed., *The American Environment,* Wesley Publishing Co., 1976.

Primack, Joel and Frank von Hippel, *Advice and Dissent: Scientists in the Political Arena,* Basic Books, Inc., 1974.

Articles

Audubon, selected issues.

Environmental Action, selected issues.

National Wildlife, selected Issues.

Sierra Club Bulletin, selected issues.

White, Lynn Jr., "The Ecology of Our Science," *Science 80,* November-December 1979, pp. 72-76.

Reports and Studies

Council on Environmental Quality, *Environmental Quality,* 9th annual report, Washington, D.C., 1978.

Editorial Research Reports: "Environmental Policy," 1974 Vol. II, p. 945; "Pollution Control: Costs and Benefits," 1976 Vol. I, p. 145; "Toxic Substance Control," 1978 Vol. II, p. 741.

INDEX

DDT (dichlorodiphenyl trichloroethane) - 47-48, 55, 57, 111, 150-152
Decibel levels - 85-87, 89, 91
Defenders of Wildlife - 134
Dichlorodiphenyl trichloroethane, *See* DDT (dichlorodiphenyl trichloroethane)
Dieldrin - 48, 57
Dingell, John D., D-Mich. - 34
Dioxin - 56, 112-113
Dow Chemical - 56, 113, 115

Each Community Helps Others (ECHO) - 90
Earth Day - 139, 144
ECHO, *See* Each Community Helps Others (ECHO)
Elephants - 131-132
Emission standards - 26-27, 31, 36-40, 66-69, 141
   automobile - 24, 35, 37, 40, 42, 68-69, 141
   coal - 28, 35-36, 66-69, 77-78
   industrial - 27-29, 39, 66-67
   utility - 24, 26, 28, 66-68
Endangered species - 14, 119-121, 123-135
   alligators - 125
   bald eagles - 127
   hunting - 134
   illegal importation - 132-133
   snail darters - 130, 145
   whooping cranes - 123-124
Endangered Species Act - 14, 119-120, 124-125, 128-129, 132, 135, 141
Endrin - 48, 51
Energy Supply and Environmental Coordination Act of 1974 - 65, 141
Environmental Defense Fund - 13, 31, 152, 155
Environmental movement - 152-156
   clean air - 31-32, 64, 68
   federal lands - 11-12
   history - 146-151
   legislation - 140-142
   toxic substances - 106-107, 112-113
   wildlife - 131-135
Environmental Protection Agency (EPA) - 15, 140
   Clean Air Act - 26, 32-34, 66, 69, 107, 140
   noise control - 83, 88-89, 91-93, 95-96
   pesticide regulation - 48-49, 51-52, 56
   toxic substances regulation - 101-102, 105-111, 142
EPA, *See* Environmental Protection Agency (EPA)

FAA, *See* Federal Aviation Administration (FAA)
Federal Aviation Act of 1968 - 94
Federal Aviation Administration (FAA) - 93-94
Federal Environmental Pesticide Control Act of 1972 - 51-52, 141
Federal Food, Drug and Cosmetic Act - 107

Federal Insecticide, Fungicide and Rodenticide Act (FIFRA) of 1947 - 51-52, 107
Federal Land Policy and Management Act (FLPMA) - 13, 141
Federal lands - 3-20
   coyote control - 51, 59-60
   legislation - 12-14
   management - 9-15
   mineral exploration - 3, 9, 16-18
   public resources - 14-19
   Sagebrush Rebellion - 7-9
   Watt, James G. - 3-9, 16-17
Federal Mine Safety and Health Act of 1977 - 141
FIFRA, *See* Federal Insecticide, Fungicide and Rodenticide Act (FIFRA) of 1947
Fish and Wildlife Service - 10, 59, 119-120, 123, 127-130, 132, 150
Fisher, Joseph L., D-Va. - 154-155
FLPMA, *See* Federal Land Policy and Management Act (FLPMA)
Food and Drug Administration - 140
Friends of the Earth - 13, 31, 154
Fund of Animals - 134
Fungicides - 47-49

General Revision Act of 1891 - 12
Genetics - 150
Gorsuch, Anne M. - 15
Grand Canyon - 12, 25
Grant, Ulysses - 12
Great Lakes Water Quality Agreement of 1978 - 64

Hart, Gary, D-Colo. - 27, 123
Hayakawa, S. I. "Sam", R-Calif. - 16
Hazardous substances, *See* Toxic substances
Health issues
   acid rain - 76
   Agent Orange - 56
   air pollution - 41
   noise pollution - 84-86
   pesticides - 47, 51, 56-57
   toxic substances - 102-103, 108-109
Herbicides - 47-50, 55-56, 111-113
Herschler, Ed - 19
Hooker Chemical and Plastics Corp. - 100

Idaho - 8, 16-17
Insecticides - 47-50, 54-57
Interior Department
   Andrus, Cecil D. - 5, 14-15, 19
   federal lands - 3-4, 8-10, 15
   Watt, James G. - 3-9, 16-17, 19
   See also Bureau of Indian Affairs; Bureau of Land Management; Bureau of Mines; Fish and Wildlife Service; Office of Surface Mining; U.S. Geological Survey; Water and Power Resource Administration
Izaak Walton League - 7, 149

Pinchot, Gifford - 12
Polybrominated biphenyl, *See* PBB (polybrominated biphenyl)
Polychlorinated biphenyl, *See* PCB (polychlorinated biphenyl)
Preservationist movement - 131-135
Prevention of significant deterioration (PSD) - 26-27

Quiet Communities Act of 1978 - 88, 91
Quiet Communities program - 89-91

Randolph, Jennings, D-W.Va. - 34
RARE II, *See* Roadless Area Review and Evaluation (RARE II)
RCRA, *See* Resource Conservation and Recovery Act (RCRA) of 1976
Reagan, Ronald
  clean air - 23-24
  environmental regulation - 27-28
  pesticides - 59
Resource Conservation and Recovery Act (RCRA) of 1976 - 105-107, 109, 113, 142, 144
Rhodes, James A. - 68
Roadless Area Review and Evaluation (RARE II) - 16
Rogers, Paul G., D-Fla. - 33
Roosevelt, Theodore - 12, 126, 149
Rootworm - 53, 55

Safe Drinking Water Act of 1974 - 107, 141
Sagebrush Rebellion - 7-9, 14, 18
Santini, James D., D-Nev. - 17
The Sea Around Us (R. Carson) - 150
Sierra Club - 7, 12-13, 26, 31, 134, 148-149
Silent Spring (R. Carson) - 47, 55, 111-112, 150
Sinclair, Upton - 148, 153
Snail darters - 130, 145
Speth, Gus - 24, 68-69, 102, 155
Stafford, Robert T., R-Vt. - 34
Staggers, Harley O., D-W.Va. - 34
State Implementation Plans - 26, 37, 39-40
Steffens, Lincoln - 148, 152
Stockholm Declaration on the Human Environment - 64
Stockman, David - 33
Strip mining - 4
Sulfur dioxide - 23, 28, 35-36, 39-41, 66-67, 72, 78
Surface Mining Control and Reclamation Act of 1977 - 141
Synthetic fuels - 28-29, 31

Tarbell, Ida - 148, 152
Taylor Grazing Act of 1934 - 12
Tellico Dam - 130, 145
Toxic metals - 74, 76

Toxic substances - 99-115
  acid rain - 74, 76
  dumping - 32, 99, 105-106, 109
  pesticides, *See* Pesticides
  sources - 101-102
  waste disposal sites - 110-111, 115
Toxic substances control - 105-109, 114
Toxic Substances Control Act (TSCA) of 1976 - 105-109, 113, 142
Turner, Frederick Jackson - 148

Udall, Morris K., D-Ariz. - 5
Udall, Steward L. - 13
Union Pacific - 31
Uranium - 9, 31
Union of Concerned Scientists - 152
U.S. Chamber of Commerce - 29-31
U.S. Forest Service - 10, 12, 16, 18, 113
U.S. Geological Survey - 10
Utility emissions - 24, 26, 28, 66-68

Velsicol Chemical Corp. - 151
Vinyl chloride - 36, 103

Wallop, Malcolm, R-Wyo. - 8
Washington, George - 17
Waste disposal
  illegal dumping - 32, 99, 105-106, 109
Waste disposal sites - 110-111, 115
Water and Power Resources Administration - 10
Water Pollution Control Act of 1972 - 107, 142
Water Quality Improvement Act of 1970 - 142
Watt, James G.
  federal lands - 3-9, 16-17, 19
  Sagebrush Rebellion - 7-9
Waxman, Henry D. D-Calif. - 33
Western Governors Policy Office (WESTPO) - 19
Whooping cranes - 123-124
Wilderness Act of 1964 - 16
Wilderness preservation - 4, 16, *See also* Wildlife refuges
Wilderness Society - 13, 149
Wildlife - 119-135
  endangered species - 14, 119-121, 123-127
  Endangered Species Act - 14, 119-120, 124-125, 128-129, 132, 135
  Fish and Wildlife Coordination Act - 128
  illegal importation - 132-133
  Lacey Act of 1900 - 126, 132
  Migratory Bird Hunting Stamp Act of 1934 - 127-128
  Norbeck-Andersen Migratory Bird Conservation Act of 1929 - 127
  preservationist movement - 131-135
Wildlife Management Institute - 134